Berlitz®
Mallorca

Text by Pam Barrett
Picture Editor: Hilary Genin
Managing Editor: Tony Halliday

Berlitz POCKET GUIDE

Mallorca

First Edition 2004 (Updated 2005)

NO part of this book may be reproduced, stored in a retrieval system or transmitted in any form or means electronic, mechanical, photocopying, recording or otherwise, without prior written permission from Berlitz Publishing. Brief text quotations with use of photographs are exempted for book review purposes only.

PHOTOGRAPHY
Pam Barrett 48, 64; Chris Coe 18; Glyn Genin 6, 10, 13, 14, 16, 22, 24, 26, 27, 28, 31, 32, 43, 46, 49, 51, 57, 61, 63, 66, 67, 72, 76, 80, 84, 98, 101; Britta Jaschinski 3tcl, 9, 11, 12, 17, 21, 33, 34, 36, 37, 39, 41, 42, 44, 53, 55, 59, 60, 65, 69, 71, 74, 78, 83, 86, 67, 89, 90, 92, 94, 97, 103; Neil Schlect 2t, 8, 56, 102
Cover picture by: Glyn Genin

CONTACTING THE EDITORS
Every effort has been made to provide accurate information in this publication, but changes are inevitable. The publisher cannot be responsible for any resulting loss, inconvenience or injury. We would appreciate it if readers would call our attention to any errors or outdated information by contacting Berlitz Publishing, PO Box 7910, London SE1 1WE, England. Fax: (44) 20 7403 0290;
e-mail: berlitz@apaguide.co.uk
www.berlitzpublishing.com

Mallorca's clean waters and beautiful beaches are the biggest attraction for many visitors

Many of the traditional windmills on the Central Plain (page 67) have been renovated and put to new uses

Valldemossa's monastery (page 46) dominates the hilltop town

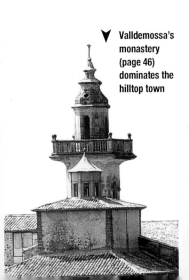

TOP TEN ATTRACTIONS

Port de Pollença (page 61) is one of the most popular family resorts in Mallorca

The Orange Tram (page 53) rattles between Sóller and its port as it has done for many decades

Deià (page 49), once the home of Robert Graves, is one of the prettiest villages on the island

Sa Calobra (page 56), a glorious bay at the end of a long and winding road

The elaborate *Moderniste* Gran Hotel (page 33) is now a cultural centre run by the Fundació La Caixa

Palma's cathedral (page 27) towers above the city and the harbour – a stunning sight if you arrive by sea

Cala Figuera (page 77) is still a working fishing port

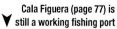

CONTENTS

A ➤ in the text denotes a highly recommended sight

INTRODUCTION

Mallorca could claim to be the perfect holiday island, blessed with attributes that entice millions of foreign visitors annually. Many of them return year after year, sometimes to the second homes they bought when they first fell in love with the island, or the boats they keep moored in one of the many harbours. The deep blue and translucent turquoise of the Mediterranean, hundreds of kilometres of coastline, secluded rocky coves and wide sandy beaches, a vibrant and sophisticated capital city, some 300 days of brilliant sunshine each year and a vast choice of accommodation and cheap flights make it irresistible.

A Varied Landscape

Lying off the northeast coast of Spain, Mallorca is the largest of the five Balearic Islands, but it is not a big place. It has more than 550km (325 miles) of coastline, but at its widest point – Cap de Sa Mola in the southwest to Capdepera in the northeast – it is only 100km (60 miles) across; at its narrowest, from the Badia d'Alcúdia in the north to the Badia de Palma in the south, it's only half that distance.

> Mallorca's beaches gained a bad reputation at one time, but after a major clean-up campaign no fewer than 28 beaches and six marinas were awarded the coveted Blue Flag for safety and cleanliness in 2000.

The landscape, however, is extremely varied. The dramatic cliffs edging the Serra de Tramuntana hug the west coast from Andratx all the way to Cap de Formentor. The coastal scenery is stunning, with dizzying drops to the sea

A sleepy street in Orient in the northwest of the island

and the tiny coves far below and picturesque villages set among centuries-old terraces. To the northwest, away from the coast, the Tramuntana range provides ideal walking and climbing conditions. There are 10 main peaks in the range, the highest of which is Puig Major at 1,445m (4,741ft). The north coast is dominated by the Bay of Alcúdia – 12km (8 miles) of fine golden sand sloping into shallow waters – and by the grassy wetlands of S'Albufera, now a protected natural park. The interior is a vast plain with sleepy towns, sandstone churches, well-tended farmland, groves of ancient olive trees and orchards of almonds and apricots. On the east coast, long sweeps of beach alternate with intimate little coves and spectacular cave formations, while several picturesque fishing harbours retain their individuality. The south centres on the cosmopolitan capital, Palma, with its splendid bay. Around it, to the east and west, spread the crowded beaches whose glorious sands first brought mass tourism to the island in the late 1950s.

A stunning view up the west coast

Vegetation, Birdlife and Climate

The flora of the island is as diverse as the landscape. There are cultivated olives, almonds, apricot and citrus trees; holm oaks and pines flourish in mountainous regions, with rosemary, lavender and heather turning the hillsides purple. There are sturdy palm trees growing at sea level, and bougainvillaea brightening village walls; and there are wild orchids and water-loving reeds, sedges and poplars in the S'Albufera marshes.

Mallorca is rich in bird-life. Come in spring, as so many birdwatchers do, to see the numerous migrants who find Mallorca a convenient stopping-off place. The Bo-quer Valley, near Pollença, is

Lemons ripe for picking

popular with those in the know. S'Albufera, on the north coast, plays host to numerous resident and migrant species, including the cattle egrets that can be seen standing on the backs of cows, pecking insects from their hides, and birds such as Eleanor's falcons that spend the summer here. Among the most colourful and exotic birds that can be seen in many locations in summer are bee-eaters and hoopoes. The island of Cabrera and the Parc Natural de Mondragó in the southeast corner are among the best places to spot migrating seabirds.

Mallorca's climate is heavenly for northern Europeans. Although summer extremes of 34ºC (93ºF) can be uncom-fortable, the July–August average is a pleasant 24º (76ºF); winters are mild and not too wet, and even the timid can swim in the sea from June to October.

The Islanders and Their Language

The population of Mallorca is approximately 628,000, of whom more than half – 325,000 – live in the capital. The rest

Catching up on the news

are distributed across 53 municipal districts, with the interior plain being the most sparsely populated region. In the peak summer season, tourists – some 9 million a year, mostly German and English – and hordes of seasonal workers, many from Andalusia, swell the population and strain the infrastructure and water supply to their limits.

Mallorcans are bilingual in Spanish and in Mallorquí, a variant of Catalan, which is now the official language. Most signs and street names are written in Mallorquí, and this is the language people choose to speak among themselves, and which is used in schools. However, they are a communicative people, quite happy to address outsiders in Castilian (Spanish), and the high number of seasonal workers from the mainland ensures that Spanish is spoken everywhere.

The Tourist Boom

Mallorca was one of the first places in Spain to be developed for tourism in the 1950s. Ever since, it has been one of the major centres, and tourism is now responsible for nearly 90 percent of the island's income. But the industry has had contradictory effects. Income from it made this region Spain's wealthiest per capita, but the environmental and psychological effects of being Europe's low-budget playground have taken a heavy toll. Four decades after it exploded, tourism overheated, leaving a forest of towering hotels and beach-hugging villa communities, whole resorts lined with fast-food outlets, tourist tat shops and loud clubs and bars serving dangerously cheap alcohol, with the big 'M' of McDonald's looming over the commercial centres.

A New Image

In the 1990s, the island government realised it was time to reassess Mallorca's tourism industry. Fearing that massive over-development and the increasingly bad reputation earned by the raucous behaviour of some visitors, as well as new trends in international tourism, were leaving the Balearics behind, the authorities took action. Moves were made to protect the remaining undeveloped areas as nature preserves, proclaiming them off-limits to construction, and demolishing some of the more unsightly hotel complexes. Almost one third of the island is now under some kind of protection order, and the advantages to the landscape and wildlife are palpable.

Magaluf was among the first of the large-scale resorts

Can Joan de S'Aigo, Miró's favourite café

There have also been energetic moves to encourage a more up-market and environmentally friendly kind of tourism. The government's *agroturisme* initiative, which promotes accommodation in small rural hotels and *fincas* (farmhouses) has been extremely popular, both with visitors looking for peace and quiet amid scenic surroundings, and farming families who were struggling to keep their properties going *(see page 106 for details)*.

Walking paths have been opened up and clearly marked, and a number of hilltop sanctuaries provide rest and respite for walkers; natural parks are widely promoted and user-friendly; and considerable investment has gone into golf courses and marinas, to attract higher income tourists and improve the environment.

In Palma de Mallorca, walking tours around the convents, patios, palaces and waterfront encourage visitors to appreciate the city's heritage, while the diversity and the quality of the capital's many museums and cultural centres would be pretty impressive in a city twice the size.

Enjoying the Island

Throughout the island, summer music festivals are held in beautiful historic buildings, attracting internationally known performers, while traditional, local festivals are also being promoted as a way of disseminating the rural culture of the Balearics. There has also been a renewed interest of late in Mallorcan food, *cuina Mallorquina*, and many venues, from the traditional *cellers (see page 70)* to smart restaurants and more basic establishments are finding that local people and foreign visitors alike are enjoying what they have to offer.

Mallorca is not a difficult place to get around. Obviously, hiring a car gives you most freedom, and this is relatively inexpensive and stress free, as most roads (except the stretch around the Bay of Palma) don't get too busy, even in summer, and parking (once you're away from the capital) is not a huge problem. But public transport is good, too, with regular buses from Palma to most points of interest, and two railway lines – one of which makes the scenic journey on the narrow-gauge line to Sóller *(see page 52)*. For another aspect of the island, you can take boat trips round many parts of the coast.

With all this going for it, Mallorca cannot be regarded as simply a place for sun, sea and sand holidays – but there is no denying that sun, sea and sand are still excellent reasons to come here.

You'll encounter people in traditional dress at village festivals

A BRIEF HISTORY

Many influences have shaped Mallorca over the past 4000 years and helped make it the fascinating place it is today. The stone towers called *talayots* that can still be seen in parts of the island were defensive structures built by early inhabitants, who are believed to have made settlements here around 1300BC. Even before that, neolithic islanders had graduated from cave dwellings to simple stone houses and cleared fields by piling stones into dividing walls – the origins of the intricate dry-stone walls called *parets seques* or *margers* that can still be seen in the island interior.

Over the centuries, the inhabitants traded with the Phoenicians, Carthaginians and Greeks, and the Carthaginians gradually colonised the islands (c. 400BC), absorbed them

The *talayotic* settlement at Ses Païsses

into their trading empire and founded the main ports. But by 123BC the Romans, who had pacified most of Spain, despatched an invading force to conquer the islands, which they named Balearis Major (Mallorca) and Balearis Minor (Menorca).

> **The early inhabitar** **skill with stones was** **evident in their dead** **use of the slingshot. T** he **'Balearic slingers' were** **renowned throughout** **the Mediterranean** **world and recruited by** **Hannibal to fight for the** **Carthaginians in the** **Punic Wars. The name** **Balearic probably comes** **from the Greek word,** *ballein*, **'to throw'.**

Romans, Vandals and Moorish Occupation

The Romans introduced Christianity, built roads and established the towns of Palmaria (Palma) and Pollentia (near Alcúdia), but during the 5th century AD, as the Roman Empire crumbled, Goths, Vandals and Visigoths poured into the Balearics. The Vandals destroyed almost all evidence of Roman occupation – the remains of Pollentia outside Alcúdia are among the very few traces left – before they were ousted in AD534 by a Byzantine expedition from Constantinople.

But more invaders were to follow. Ignited by the teachings of the Prophet Mohammed, Islam spread like wildfire in the 8th century. A Moorish army led by General Tarik landed on the Iberian peninsula in 711 and in just seven years, most of Spain was under Moorish rule. While the Balearics remained submissive, the *caliphs* (rulers) were content to accept tribute from them, but local disturbances prompted an invasion at the beginning of the 10th century. Both islands were conquered and became part of the Caliphate of Córdoba.

Although little Moorish architecture remains – the Arab Baths in Palma and the Jardins d'Alfàbia near Sóller are two

The Banys Àrabs in Palma

exceptions – the influence can be seen in Palma, in the Palau de l'Almudaina, in the fountains in S'Hort del Rei, and in many shady patios. Some place names are also of Arabic origin – Alcúdia (Al-Kudia) means 'on the hill', and Binissalem means 'son of peace'.

The Reconquest

The aim of the crusades in Spain was the eviction of the Muslims. After the recovery of Jerusalem in 1099, it took 400 years of sieges and battles, treaties and betrayals before Christian rulers succeeded in subduing the Moors. In 1229, a Catalan army led by King Jaume I of Aragón and Catalunya took Mallorca. Jaume proved to be an enlightened ruler who profited from the talents of the Moors – those who remained were forcibly converted to Christianity – as well as those of the large Jewish and Genoese trading communities.

Jaume I reigned in Aragón for six decades, but he made the mistake of dividing between his sons the lands he had united. Initially this resulted in the Independent Kingdom of Mallorca, first under Jaume II, then under Sanxo and Jaume III. But dynastic rivalry triggered the overthrow of the latter by his cousin, Pere IV. Attempting to make a comeback, Jaume III was killed in battle near Llucmajor in 1349.

In the following century the Catholic Monarchs, Ferdinand and Isabella, leading a unified Spain, completed the Reconquest, taking Granada, the only Moorish enclave left on the peninsula, in 1492.

The Spanish Empire

As one tumultuous age ended, another began. Christopher Columbus (Cristobal Colón), the seafaring captain from Genoa (whom at least three Mallorcan towns claim as their own), believed he could reach the East Indies by sailing westwards. In the same year that Granada fell, Columbus crossed the Atlantic. Spain exported its adventurers, traders and priests, and imposed its language, culture and religion on the New World, creating a vast empire in the Americas. Ruthless, avaricious conquistadors extracted and sent back incalculable riches in silver and gold. The century and a half after 1492 was known as Spain's Golden Age, but it carried the seeds of its own decline. Plagued by corruption and incompetence, and drained of manpower and ships by such adventurism as the dispatch of the ill-fated Armada against England in 1588, Spain was unable to defend her expansive interests. The Balearics did not benefit much from the glory years. They were forbidden to trade with the New World, and their existing trade on the eastern routes was interrupted by marauding pirates based in North Africa, as well as by the powerful Turkish fleet.

Jaume I, who captured Mallorca in 1229

Fernando and Isabella greet Christopher Columbus

Wars and Consequences

The daughter of Ferdinand and Isabella married the heir to the Holy Roman Emperor, Maximilian of Habsburg. The Spanish crown duly passed to the Habsburgs and remained in their hands until the feeble-minded Carlos II died in 1700, leaving no heir. France seized the chance to install the young grandson of Louis XIV on the Spanish throne. A rival Habsburg claimant was supported by Austria and Britain, who saw a powerful Spanish-French alliance as a major threat. In the subsequent War of the Spanish Succession (1702–13) most of the kingdom of Aragón, including the Balearics, backed the Habsburgs. Britain seized Menorca and retained it, under the Treaty of Utrecht, when the war was over.

By 1805, Spain was once more aligned with France, and Spanish ships fought alongside the French against Admiral Lord Nelson at the Battle of Trafalgar. But Napoleon came to distrust his Spanish ally and forcibly replaced the king of Spain with his own brother, Joseph Bonaparte. A French army marched in to subdue the country. The Spanish resisted and, aided by British troops commanded by the Duke of Wellington, drove the French out. What the British call the Peninsular War (1808–14) is known in Spain as the War of Independence.

During the 19th century, most of Spain's possessions in the Americas broke away. The Balearics, further neglected, were beset with poverty and thousands of islanders emigrated to South America in search of a better life. A brief upturn, due to the successful trade in wine, ended when the phylloxera louse destroyed the island's vines.

Crises, Republic and Civil War

The beginning of the 20th century in Spain was marked by social and political crises, assassinations and near anarchy. The colonial war in Morocco provided a distraction, but a disastrous defeat there in 1921 led to a coup and the dictatorship of General Primo de Rivera. He fell in 1929, and when elections of 1931 revealed massive anti-royalist feeling, the king followed him into exile.

The new republic was conceived amid an outbreak of strikes and uprisings. In February 1936 the left-wing Popular Front won a majority of seats in the Cortes (parliament), but across Spain localised violence displaced debate. In July 1936, General Francisco Franco staged a coup, which was supported by the military, monarchists, conservatives, the clergy and the right-wing Falangist movement. Aligned on

Creative Input

Mallorca has always attracted creative people. In 1838 Frédéric Chopin and George Sand spent several months in Valldemossa, during which he composed *The Raindrop Prelude* and she wrote *A Winter in Majorca*. Catalan poet and painter Santiago Rusiñol spent some time in Deià at the turn of the 20th century; and poet and author Robert Graves came to the village in 1929 and made it his home. He was buried in the little churchyard on the hill in 1985; his son, Tomás, still lives on the island. Artist Joan Miró, whose wife Pilar was Mallorcan, set up house and studio in Palma in 1956, rather than live under the Franco regime and he, too, stayed until his death (in 1983).

the Republican government's side were liberals, socialists, communists and anarchists. The ensuing Spanish Civil War (1936–39) was brutal and bitter. Support for both sides poured in from outside Spain. Those on the Republican side believed it was a contest between democracy and dictatorship, while Nationalist supporters saw it as a battle between order and communist chaos. During the three years the war lasted, around one million Spaniards lost their lives.

Mallorca and Menorca found themselves on opposite sides. Menorca declared for the Republic, and stayed with it to the bitter end. Mallorca's garrison seized the island for the Nationalists. Early in the war, the Republicans used their one battleship to support an invasion of Mallorca, but it ended in failure. A decisive factor was the presence in Palma of Italian air squadrons, used to bomb Republican Barcelona.

New Horizons

Exhausted after the Civil War, Spain remained on the sidelines during World War II and, after the dark years of isolation known as the *Noche Negra* (Black Night), began a slow economic recovery under Franco's oppressive, law-and-order regime, boosted by the growth of the tourism industry.

A small élite had visited the island in the 1920s, but it was in the late 1950s and early 1960s that northern Europeans began making sun-seeking pilgrimages to Spain, and the Balearic Islands, in any numbers. Tourism transformed the impoverished country's economy, landscape and society. Eager to capitalise, government and private interests poured everything into mass tourism, triggering a rash of uncontrolled and indiscriminate building, with scant regard for tradition or aesthetics. Almost as influential as the financial input, to a country that had for so long been cut off from the rest of Europe, was the injection of foreign influences, particularly those associated with the liberalism of the 1960s.

Mallorca, once dependent on agriculture, fishing and small local industries, experienced an explosive growth in tourism and swiftly became one of Europe's most popular holiday destinations.

After Franco's death in 1975, his designated successor, the grandson of Alfonso XIII, was crowned King Juan Carlos I. To the dismay of Franco diehards, the king managed a smooth transition to democracy, then stood back to allow it full rein, as he continues to do today. After decades of repression, new freedoms and autonomy were granted to Spanish regions and their languages and cultures enjoyed a long-sought renaissance. The Balearic Islands were granted a degree of autonomy in 1978 and five years later became the Comunidad Autónoma de las Islas Baleares. Mallorquí was recognised officially as the language of Mallorca.

The Spanish and Balearic flags fly side by side

Street music is a part of many traditional occasions

Modernisation

Spain joined the European Community (now the European Union) in 1986, which gave a further boost to an expanding economy. Mallorca's tourist industry continued to grow but so did a realisation that lack of planning and good taste were leading to damaging long-term consequences – to the environment and to the island's reputation. By the late 1990s, when the lager lout image had become too closely associated with some resorts, production of domestic waste was double the national average and electricity consumption had increased by 37 percent in five years, a new emphasis on quality tourism and safeguarding the environment had taken root *(see page 11)*. Building restrictions were implemented, a number of areas were declared protected zones, and environmental groups lobbied the government in areas where they felt protection was most needed.

In May 2002, after two years of argument, the *ecotasa* (eco-tax) came into effect – a small per capita tax on hotel guests. The revenue went into a Tourist Area Restoration Fund to improve the Balearic Islands' ecology and help fund urban restoration. However, after more wrangling and a shift to the right in island politics, the tax was discontinued at the end of 2003. It is to be hoped, though, that a new environmental awareness, and legislation to back it up, has come just in time to preserve the natural beauty, the distinctive character and friendly atmosphere of this lovely island.

Historical Landmarks

c. 1300BC Megalithic Talayotic culture; stone towers, *talayots*, constructed.

c. 400BC Carthaginians colonise the Balearics.

123BC Romans invade; they name the island Balearis Major.

120BC–AD400 Romans establish towns, including Palmaria (Palma) and Pollentia (Alcúdia).

426 Vandals invade Balearics.

711 Moors land near Gibraltar, and Spain falls under Islamic rule.

848 Moorish rule imposed in the Balearics; it lasts for 300 years.

1229 Mallorca taken by the Christian army under Jaume I.

1285–87 Alfonso III of Aragón captures Palma.

1349 Jaume III killed in battle by Pere IV of Aragón, ending the Independent Kingdom of Mallorca.

1492 Spain united under the Catholic Monarchs.

1554 Palma fortified to protect it from pirate attacks.

1713 Juníper Serra, founder of the Californian missions, born in Petra.

1837 First steamship service links Mallorca and Spanish mainland.

1936–39 Spanish Civil War. Mallorca seized by Nationalist forces.

1936–75 Franco's dictatorship; the early years are typified by economic hardship.

1960 Mallorca's airport built. Tourism begins to replace agriculture as the island's main source of income.

1975 Juan Carlos I becomes king after the death of Franco.

1978 Statute of Autonomy gives the Balearic Islands a degree of autonomy; five years later they become an autonomous province and Catalan/Mallorquí is restored as the official language.

1986 Spain joins the European Community (now European Union).

1996 The government of the Balearic Islands initiates measures to protect the environment and encourage eco-friendly tourism.

2002 The euro becomes the official currency. An eco-tax is imposed to help finance environmental measures but is discontinued in 2003.

2004 PSOE (Socialist Party) comes to power in March elections in Spain, but Partido Popular (PP) is dominant in the government of the Balearic Islands.

WHERE TO GO

Although some visitors to this small Mediterranean island arrive by ferry from mainland Spain, the vast majority land at Palma's huge airport, Son Sant Joan, about 11km (7 miles) outside the capital, Palma de Mallorca. A ring road – the Via Cintura – skirts the city, with good roads radiating off to the rest of the island; to the craggy, beautiful northwest coast, the quiet, friendly towns of the interior plain, the wetlands of S'Albufera in the north, the tiny *calas* in the east, and the tourist-dominated strips to the east and west of Palma and along the north coast.

Tour companies offer excursions, by coach or boat, or a combination of the two, to mountain villages, hidden beaches, spectacular caves and weekly markets, but hiring a car *(see page 110)* is the best way to get around. There are only two railway lines – one goes to Inca, in the centre of the island, the other is the picturesque route to Sóller *(see page 52),* but bus services throughout Mallorca are comprehensive and reliable *(see page 123),* although public transport obviously gives you less freedom than a hired car.

PALMA DE MALLORCA

Set around a sheltered bay, Palma is a large, cosmopolitan city, with around 325,000 inhabitants – over half the permanent population of Mallorca. It is very much a Mediterranean city, with palm trees and bushes of fragrant oleander, outdoor cafés with colourful awnings, and yachts bobbing in the bay among working vessels. Palma is a city with a long history, too, as the Gothic cathedral towering above the city walls indicates as you approach from the airport. It's smart

Port de Pollença has something for everyone

and urbane, with chic designer boutiques and contemporary art galleries hidden in narrow alleys. And it's a city that stays awake late at night. Every visitor should try to spend a whole day here, at least, but it really merits a longer stay.

The old quarter surrounding the cathedral – 'Centre Historic' on direction signs – sits on a small hill overlooking the bay, and its narrow, atmospheric streets are full of pleasant surprises. To the east of the centre is the Platja de Palma, a long line of excellent sandy beaches that have been defaced by a sad stretch of concrete from Ca'n Pastilla to S'Arenal. To the west is the seaside promenade of modern Palma, where luxury hotels look out over a forest of masts in the yacht harbour, although divided from it by a stretch of six-lane highway. Crowning the wooded slopes above the city, where the Spanish royal family have a summer home, are the stone towers of the Castell de Bellver (see page 38).

Palma's cathedral keeps watch over the harbour

The Cathedral

Standing proudly above the city walls, spectacular when illuminated at night, is Palma's **cathedral** (open Mon–Fri 10am–6.15pm, Sat 10am–2.15pm; entrance fee; entered via the museum). Also known as **La Seu**, this is one of the finest Gothic churches in Spain. It was begun in 1230, by Jaume I, on the site of the Great Mosque after the Christians recaptured the island from the Moors, but took nearly

An exterior detail of the cathedral

four centuries to complete. Densely packed flying buttresses on the south front create an extraordinary effect, especially in the glow of the setting sun when they cast their reflection in the lake of the Parc de la Mar below.

The 14th-century **Portal del Mirador** on this same front is a feast of carved stone figurines by architect and sculptor Guillem Sagrera (1397–1454), including a depiction of the Last Supper. The Portal Major, the neo-Gothic west door, is less interesting; access through the north door, the Portal de l'Almoina, below the square 13th-century bell tower, is reserved for those attending mass. Before you go inside, stop to admire the splendid view of the Badia de Palma from the observation point known as the **Mirador** to the south.

The **Museu del Catedral**, through which you enter the cathedral, contains a splendid silver monstrance, some interesting medieval paintings and holy relics. Sections of the original Roman city can be seen through a glass floor. An early Renaissance doorway in carved stone leads you into

The Palau de l'Almudaina was home to medieval kings

the baroque Chapter House. The vault of the cathedral's three-aisled, 121-m (396-ft) interior is supported by slim, elegant pillars. The largest of the seven **rose windows** is magnificent, 12m (40ft) across and composed of 1,236 separate sections of stained glass. The extraordinary *baldachino*, a wrought-iron crown of thorns over the high altar, was added by Catalan *Moderniste* architect Antoni Gaudí, creator of Barcelona's unfinished Sagrada Família, who worked for some 10 years on the cathedral in the early 20th century. (*Modernisme* is the Catalan version of Art Nouveau.) In the Capella de la Trinitá at the east end of the church are the tombs of Jaume II and Jaume III, 14th-century kings of Catalunya and Mallorca.

Palau de l'Almudaina

The **Palau de l'Almudaina** (open Mon–Fri 10am–6.30pm, Sat 10am–2pm; entrance fee) stands to the west of the cathedral. Once the residence of the Moorish vizirs, then of the medieval kings of Mallorca, it is a perfect blend of Islamic and Catalan-Gothic architecture. There is a stone-vaulted, 13th-century throne room (the Tinell), a pretty courtyard (Patio del Rei), a Gothic chapel (Capella de Santa Anna), and heavily restored royal offices, sometimes used by the present king, where traces of early paintwork survive on the ceilings and walls. There are also some impressive 15th- and 16th-century Flemish tapestries.

The 18-m (58-ft) **Arc de la Drassana Musulmana** spanning the water in S'Hort del Rei below *(see page 36)* once gave the Moorish rulers direct access to the sea.

Around the Historic Centre

In Carrer Palau Reial, to the north of the Almudaina, where brightly painted horse-drawn carriages wait for customers, is another splendid palace, in which the **Palau March Museu** (open Apr–Oct: Mon–Fri 10–6.30pm; Nov–Mar: till 6pm; Sat 10am–2pm all year; entrance fee) opened in 2003. Within this majestic building and its courtyard a superb collection of contemporary sculpture has been gathered, including works by Henry Moore, Barbara Hepworth, Rodin and Chillida, and murals by the Catalan artist Josep Maria Sert, as well as high-quality temporary exhibitions. The palace is also used as a venue for classical concerts in July and August *(see page 93)*.

The ochre colonnades of the Parliament Building – **Parlament de les Illes Baleares** – run almost the length of Carrer Palau Reial. At the far end, the opulent Renaissance façade of the **Ajuntament** (Town Hall), its overhanging wooden roof supported by carved beams, dominates the **Plaça del Cort**. In the centre of the little square is an ancient, gnarled olive tree, a favourite spot for photos.

Turn right from the *plaça* and you will reach the 14th-century church of **Santa Eulàlia**, with altar paintings by

Francisco Gomez and several baroque chapels. Behind the church in the narrow Carrer Sanç is **Can Joan de S'Aigo**, a beautifully tiled café, founded in 1700, which was artist Joan Miró's favourite place for hot chocolate and almond cake.

Nearby, shaded by palms and plane trees, the Plaça Quadrado has a number of attractive *Moderniste* buildings, the best one being Can Barceló (1902). Above the third-storey oriel windows the façade is decorated with mosaics portraying domestic scenes with women and children.

The adjoining Plaça Sant Francesc is dominated by the **Basílica de Sant Francesc** (open Mon–Sat 9.30am–12.30pm, 3.30–6pm, Sun 9.30am–12.30pm; free), founded by Jaume I in 1232. A sculpture outside depicts Mallorcan missionary, Fray Juníper Serra, the founder of the first Californian missions *(see page 69)*. A chapel on the left-hand side of the gloomy interior contains the alabaster tomb of the Catalan scholar, mystic and missionary, Ramón Llull (1235–1316). But the main event is the enchanting late-Gothic cloister, with slender columns, delicate tracery and lemon trees around a central fountain.

For details of guided tours of Palma's patios, which take place between 23 June and 30 August, tel: 971 711 547, or go to the Visitors' Centre, Carrer Sant Roc 4, Mon–Fri 10am–1.30pm, 4.30–7.30pm. There are daily tours, but those in English are usually on Tuesday and Thursday.

Patios and Museums

The old quarter of Palma is rich in baronial mansions, mostly dating from the 16th to 18th centuries, with wonderful patios behind their great wooden doors. With ornate staircases, decorated tiles, palms and potted plants, sometimes cooled by small fountains, they are a delight. Among the best are Can Olesa on Carrer Morey,

Can Olesa has one of the most delightful patios

Can Tacón on Carrer de Sant Jaume II, and Can Bordils and Can Oms, both on Carrer Almudaina. Usually you have to be content with peeping through the gateways, but if you take a patios tour *(see box)*, then you will be allowed inside.

You can also see several of these patios by visiting the excellent museums housed within. On Carrer de la Portella, the Renaissance **Ca La Gran Cristiana** houses the **Museu de Mallorca** (open Jun–Oct: Tues–Sat 10am–2pm, 5–7pm, Thur 6–9pm, Sun 10am–2pm; Nov–May: 9.30am–1.30pm, 4–6pm, Sun 10am–2pm; entrance fee). The museum's four floors span Mallorca's history, from the *talyotic* period, through the Romans, Moors and Christians, coming up to date with *Moderniste* tiles and furniture and later 20th-century paintings and sculpture, among them works by Mallorcan Expressionist, Juli Ramis (1909–90).

Another splendid mansion with a patio in Carrer de la Portella is home to one of Palma's newer museums, the

Casa Museu Torrents Lladó (open Tues–Fri 10am–6pm, Sat 11am–2pm; entrance fee). The beautifully furnished home and studio of the 20th-century Catalan portraitist and landscape painter is fascinating, and houses an eclectic selection of his work and memorabilia.

If you're keen for more, go to **Can Marquès** (open Mon–Fri 10am–3pm; Sun groups of 30+ only; entrance fee), in nearby Carrer Zanglada, the only mansion whose interior can be visited. You have to take a guided tour, but individual visitors are welcome and don't have to wait. Originally 15th-century, the house is mostly furnished and decorated in bourgeois, 19th-century style, with some interesting *Moderniste* additions, and the tour illuminates the lifestyle of an upper-class Mallorquin family of the period.

The three museums above, plus the Museu de la Catedral and the **Museu Diocesà** (open Mon–Sat 10am–1pm, 4.30–7pm; entrance fee) can be visited on a combined ticket, which, at €10, represents a considerable saving. The permanent home of the Museu Diocesà is in the Episcopal Palace, but while this is closed for lengthy renovation work, the best of the collection is housed at Carrer Calders (Plaça Sant Jeroní).

Forn des Teatre, a famous café

Ancient and Modern

After visiting the museums, you could pop into the nearby **Banys Àrabs** (Arab Baths; open Apr–Sept: daily 9.30am–8pm; Oct–Mar: 9.30am–6pm; entrance fee) on Carrer Can Serra, still standing after 1,000 years. The courtyard garden is a tranquil and beautiful place when it's not filled with excursion groups. Late afternoon is usually a good time to go.

Alternatively, retrace your steps to the Plaça Cort, from where it's a short distance up the intriguing little shopping streets of Carrer Colom and Carrer Jaume II to the deep yellow façades and green shutters of the former market place, the **Plaça Major**. The square is busy with cafés, street entertainers and handicraft stalls selling some rather good jewellery and batik work. Escalators lead down to a subterranean shopping mall and public toilets.

The *Moderniste* Gran Hotel is now a cultural centre

On the approach to the square is the **Plaça Marquès del Palmer** where, sandwiched among chic leather shops and a good bookshop, are two excellent examples of *Moderniste* architecture – Can Forteza Rei and L'Àguila, adorned with ornate iron grillwork and colourful ceramic flourishes.

Down a flight of steps from the Plaça Major, lined with tourist-trap kiosks, is Plaça Weyler, with two more fine examples of *Modernisme*. The major one is the imposing **Gran Hotel**, now run as a cultural centre by the **Fundació La Caixa** (open Tues–Sat 10am–9pm, Sun 10am–2pm; free). It includes a good bookshop, a smart café/restaurant (open Mon–Sat 9am–10pm, Sun 9am–2pm) and an art centre which stages exhibitions of contemporary art and has

The sinuous lines of Can Casayas

a permanent display of the work of Catalan painter Hermen Anglada Camarasa (1872–1959), who lived in Pollença. This was the first modern hotel in Mallorca, built in 1903 by the Catalan Lluís Doménech i Muntaner. After a chequered history it was acquired in 1987 by La Caixa, a savings bank that does a lot for the arts in Catalunya and the Balearics.

Across from the Gran Hotel is a small bakery and café, the **Forn des Teatre**, whose graceful façade graces many a postcard. Down the street, on Plaça Mercat, stand the two gently undulating *Moderniste* buildings that comprise **Can Casayas**. The bakery got its name from the neighbouring Teatre Principal, which was once a grand edifice, and no doubt will be again, but is at present undergoing extensive renovation. Follow the road past the theatre and you reach **Via Roma**, an avenue lined with plane trees and flower stalls that is called La Rambla, after Barcelona's promenade, but has neither the architecture nor the buzz of its Catalan namesake.

Barrí Sant Miquel

Turn right from Plaça Major, instead of descending the steps, and you will be in Carrer Sant Miquel, a busy pedestrianised shopping street, where the **Museu d'Art Espanyol Contem-**

porani (open Mon–Fri 10am–6.30pm, Sat 10am–1.30pm; entrance fee) houses a collection belonging to the wealthy March banking family in a striking building with marble staircases and good stained glass. The 70-strong permanent collection includes works by Picasso, Miró, Dalí and Juan Gris. Next door to the museum, the Banco March is open for business in a marble-pillared, wood-panelled setting.

Heading north up the street you will come to the church of **Sant Antoniet** (open Mon–Fri 10am–1.30pm, 5–8pm, Sat 10am–1.30pm), deconsecrated and now used as an exhibition space for installation art and a variety of exhibitions. A little further down is the church of **Sant Miquel** (open Mon–Sat 8.30am–1pm, 5–7pm, Sun 10am–1.30pm, 5.30–7pm), where the first Mass after the Christian reconquest was celebrated. This ancient church is the religious heart of the neighbourhood, a solid building with a fine baroque altarpiece.

The March Dynasty

The Fundació March was set up by the extremely wealthy March banking dynasty in 1955 as a philanthropic institution to promote science and culture. You will see branches of the Banca March all over the Balearic Islands, and notice their name appended to numerous cultural ventures. As well as the two major museums mentioned here, there is an extensive library and archive in the Palau March, also open to the public, and concerts are held there in summer. The foundation also funds an annual programme of 20th-century classical music at Palma's Auditorio and summer concerts in the Jardins March in Cala Ratjada *(see page 93)*, where there is some splendid modern sculpture. Annual prizes for literary criticism and short novels are also awarded by a dynasty that obviously believes in putting a lot back into the community on which its wealth was founded.

Further up, on the right, is the **Mercat de l'Olivar** (open daily), the city's largest fish, meat and produce market. A short distance further on is the Plaça d'Espanya, where you will find the railway station and the main bus terminal.

Passeig des Born to Sa Llotja

If you go west instead of north from Plaça Weyler, along the traffic-filled Carrer Unió, you will come to Plaça Rei Joan Carles I. Ahead is the busy shopping street, Avinguda Jaume III; to your left, the leafy **Passeig des Born**, its broad central avenue, lined with benches, guarded at either end by stone sphinxes, runs down to the **Plaça de la Reina**, a large central fountain. At No. 27, the 18th-century **Palau Solleric** (open Tues–Sat 10am–2pm, 5–9pm, Sun 10am–1.30pm) houses a cultural foundation, hosts art exhibitions and has a café and bookshop.

To the left of Plaça de la Reina (past the tourist office, *see page 126*) steps lead up to the cathedral, where we began. Hugging the old city walls is **S'Hort del Rei**, a lovely Arabic-style garden, with fountains and pools, which makes a pleasant distraction from city traffic. Miró's beloved **Personatge** sculpture (known as 'The Egg') stands on the corner

Miró's Personatge sculpture

nearest the *plaça*. Facing it is the new, cool and minimalist café that is part of the Palau March *(see page 29)*. Below the walls on the southern (sea) side, and adjacent to Avinguda Antoni Maura, the attractively landscaped Parc de la Mar, with an artificial lake and modern sculpture, forms a good barrier against the coastal motorway, the **Passeig Marítim**.

Many hours can be whiled away at Palma's outdoor cafés

A right turn here (where a statue of the mystic Ramón Llull stands on a traffic island) leads to the turreted **Sa Llotja** (open Mon–Fri 11am–2pm, 5–9pm when exhibitions are on; free), in the square of the same name. It was designed in the 15th century by Guillem Sagrera (after whom this stretch of the Passeig Marítim is named). Once the merchants' stock exchange, it is now used for art exhibitions and is one of Spain's finest civic Gothic buildings. Slim columns twist through a light and airy interior to the vaulted roof. Nearby, in **Plaça Drassana**, a pleasant neighbourhood square, a cannon and anchor stand outside the 17th-century **Consolat de Mar**, the former maritime law court. The grassy stretch between the two buildings is bordered by the Porta del Mar, one of the old city gates. The maze of narrow streets between Plaça de Sa Llotja and Plaça de la Reina form Palma's restaurant and nightlife area where you can find eating and drinking places of all kinds *(see pages 96 and 137)*.

The Waterfront

Cross the road at the nearest traffic lights to explore Palma's harbour and waterfront, in all its diversity. There are fishermen mending their nets (although the fishing fleet is not what it was), smart yachts around the **Real Club Náutic**, a tiny fishermen's chapel, Sant Elm, opportunities to take trips around the harbour, and, at the western end, the ferry passenger terminal. En route, several cafés and restaurants overlook the port, while cyclists, runners and roller-bladers whizz past on a designated track. The harbour front is planted with palms, hibiscus and oleander, but there is no getting away from the fact that six lanes of traffic are roaring past on the other side. Despite this, it is very pleasant on a summer evening, when the sun is setting over the water and there's a great view of the illuminated cathedral.

To the west of the city is the prestigious **Es Baluard Museu d'Art Modern i Contemporani** (open Jun–Sept: daily 10am–midnight; Oct–May: Tues–Sun 10am–8pm; entrance fee), which opened in 2004 in a stunning white building in Plaça Porta de Santa Catalina. Its modern and contemporary displays include work by Picasso, Miró, Tàpies and Barceló.

Three Out of Town Attractions

Further west are three more places worth mentioning. The **Poble Espanyol** (open Apr–Oct: daily 9am–7pm; Nov–Mar: 9am–6pm; entrance fee), a walled town of replica architectural treasures from across Spain, is kitsch but entertaining nonetheless. The buildings house shops, craft studios, bars and cafés. It is reached on bus No. 5 from the Plaça d'Espanya.

Just south of the Poble Espanyol, perched on a hilltop, is the **Castell de Bellver** (open Apr–Sept: Mon–Sat 8am–8.30pm, Sun 10am–7pm; Oct–Mar: 8am–7.15pm, Sun 10am–5pm; entrance fee). Get bus No. 3 from Plaça Rei Joan

Carles to the Plaça Gomilla, from where it's a 1-km (½-mile) walk. A magnificent example of Gothic military architecture, the castle has commanded the approaches to the city since the early 14th century. From the circular battlements the view of the city and the sweep of the bay is stunning. Inside, the small **Museu d'Història de la Ciutat** (closed Sunday) traces the history and archaeology of the area.

The best of the three is the **Fundació Pilar i Joan Miró** (open May–Sept: Tues–Sat 10am–7pm; Oct–Apr: 10am–6pm; Sun 10am–3pm all year; entrance fee) in Carrer Joan de Saridakis in the suburb of Cala Major. Bus No. 4 from Plaça de la Reina will take you right to the door. The Catalan artist and his Mallorcan wife lived on the island from 1956 until his death in 1983, and the foundation, in a streamlined white building designed by Rafael Moneo and surrounded by gardens and ponds, displays a fine selection of his work.

The Passeig Marítim runs along the waterfront

THE WESTERN CORNER

When tourism hit Mallorca, the Bay of Palma, with two magnificent sweeps of white sand almost 30km (18 miles) long, was irresistible, and the resorts that mushroomed along here in the 1960s and 1970s gave the island a name for cheap and cheerful holidays. The picture soon turned decidedly tacky, dominated by down-market package tourism and high-rise concrete hotels.

To the west of the bay, things start getting better after Camp de Mar, where the coast road winds through forest to Port d'Andratx. After a detour to Sant Elm, out on the island's southwestern tip, there is a beautiful winding coast road to the village of Banyalbufar before heading inland, via the country estate of La Granja and La Reserva Puig de Galatzó, after which you can complete the circle back to Palma, or carry on up the picturesque west coast. For the southern end of the bay, *see page 78.*

For an underwater adventure, take a 50-minute trip on the Nemo Submarine from Magaluf. There's lots of underwater life to see and it's very comfortable and well organised, if a bit expensive. Tours every hour, Mar–Oct: 9am–5pm; advance booking necessary, tel: 971 130 244, or go to Carrer Galeón 2, Magaluf.

West of the Bay

If you don't want to visit the resorts, take the Via Cintura (ring road) in the direction of Andratx as you go west along Palma's seafront; otherwise, take the coast road. You could turn off to **Cala Major** (where the Spanish royal family have their summer home) to visit the Fundació Miró *(see page 39)* if you did not incorporate it in your Palma itinerary. The road then runs through the resorts of **Sant Agustí**, with a small yacht harbour, and crowded **Ses Illetes**, to a rocky stretch of coast and the exclusive **Bendinat** and **Portals Nous**. Here, apartment blocks cluster on the slopes and an ambitious and glamorous marina, **Puerto Portals**, has been carved out of the cliffs. All very classy.

Get to Magaluf beach early to find a shady spot

Sandy beaches start again at the resorts of **Costa d'En Blanes** – where the popular dolphinarium, **Marineland** *(see page 88),* is situated – and **Palma Nova**. The latter blends almost imperceptibly into big, brash **Magaluf**. The wide, sandy beach is a solid block of bronzing bodies by day; the town centre an equally solid stretch of drinkers by night. This is tourism overkill: vast bars and discos, restaurants offering frankfurters, curry and all-day English breakfasts, wide-screen televised football, and some of the trashiest shops imaginable.

To the south, lined by pine trees, a road goes to the pretty cove of **Portals Vells**, which has somehow escaped much development. In the cliffs are huge caverns dating from Roman times, enlarged over the centuries. Boats make the short excursion from the pier at Magaluf, so it's not always peaceful. Not far south of Portals Vells, you can walk to the tranquil cove of **Cala Figuera**, but the end of the peninsula is a military zone.

Port d'Andratx and Sant Elm

Pick up the main Andratx road at Magaluf, but turn off at Camp de Mar where a scenic road twists through pine forest to **Port d'Andratx**. More yachts than fishing boats bob on the calm waters of the bay these days. The old harbour area still looks traditional but a string of chic restaurants and shops lines it, and villas and apartments climb the slopes across the water. But the lack of a sandy beach has kept the big hotels and package tours away and Port d'Andratx feels relaxed. The impressive new **Centro Cultural Andratx** stages contemporary art exhibitions in a parkland setting (tel: 971 137 770 for details).

From the inland town of Andratx, make a detour to **Sant Elm**, the island's westernmost point, a former fishing village that has managed to retain its identity, though sailors, surfers and divers have known about it for a long time. Offshore, the

Sant Elm is a peaceful little corner of the island

nature-reserve island of **Sa Dragonera**, can be visited by boat in the summer.

Up the Scenic Coast

From Andratx the C710 runs across the southern reaches of the Serra de Tramuntana, around numerous hairpin bends to the coast, where it winds along the cliff tops. To the right of the road are ter- races planted with fruit trees

Terraced hills at Banyalbufar

and olives, and some delightful little villages. Along the road stands a succession of *miradors*, lookout points with com- manding views of the entire coast, still crowned with ancient watchtowers from which lookouts once scanned the sea for pirate ships. The **Mirador de Ricardo Roca** is one of the major ones, with fantastic views of the coast, and a huge restaurant in which to sit and enjoy them.

Estellencs, some 4km (2½ miles) on, is an ancient village, set amid orange groves on the slopes of Puig de Galatzó (1,026m/3,360ft). From the town you can walk or drive down a track to a little fishing cove. Another 5km (3 miles) further on, one of the finest views of the coast can be had from the 16th-century tower of the **Mirador de Ses Ànimes**. The next town, **Banyalbufar**, is a rather self-consciously pretty place with Moorish origins. There are a couple of pleasant hotels and several restaurants, and a lane twists down to a rocky cove and small beach.

La Granja and La Reserva

North of Banyalbufar, the road turns inland, in the direction of **Esporles**, close to which you'll find the estate of **La**

Home-grown produce is for sale at La Granja

Granja (open May–Oct: daily 10am–7pm; Nov–Apr: 10am–6pm; entrance fee). It's a bit of a theme park, but well worth a visit. The estate was renowned for the purity of its water in Roman times and there are still numerous fountains in the peaceful, leafy gardens. The interior of the huge house is magnificent and gives a good idea of how the landed classes once lived. The chapel and the torture chamber speak for themselves. The donkeys, pigs, wild goats and sheep in the grounds are usually a hit with children. On Wednesday and Friday from 3.30–5pm there are handicraft demonstrations and performances of regional music, folk dancing and dressage, and there are always tastings of fig bread and local cheese and sausages.

From here, you can return to Palma on the PM104, continue up the west coast, or take the minor road to Puigpunyent to visit **La Reserva Puig de Galatzó** (open Apr–Oct: daily 10am–7pm; Nov–Mar: 10am–6pm; last admittance 2 hours before closing; entrance fee). Some 3km (2 miles) of paths run past numerous waterfalls and caves through protected land, rich in bird and animal life, on the lush slopes of Galatzó, known as the mystical mountain because of its magnetic properties. There's also a barbecue area and a children's playground. The paths are fairly easy ones, although you will need to wear sensible shoes. If you want something more adventurous you can try abseiling, climbing, mountain biking and crossing wavy suspension bridges – although these so-called 'Adventure Trails' are quite expensive.

THE WEST COAST

This is one of the most dramatic and beautiful routes in Mallorca. It's hard to pick a highlight as there are so many, from Valldemossa, with the former monastery, where George Sand and Frédéric Chopin once stayed, to the lovely hilltop village of Deià, once home to poet Robert Graves; there's also the cliff-top mansion of the Habsburg Archduke Ludwig, and the agreeable town of Sóller.

Whether you are continuing a route round the coast on the C710 or coming direct from Palma on the PM111, a good, straightish road, running through groves of olives and almonds, your first stop will be at Valldemossa. As you approach, the incline becomes steeper and the village and monastery suddenly appear, like a fairytale settlement on a hillside.

La Real Cartuja de Valldemossa

Although **Valldemossa** was the birthplace of Mallorca's only home-grown saint, Catalina Tomás *(see below)*, it was the visit,

---

Catalina Tomás

Santa Catalina is Mallorca's very own saint. She was born in Valldemossa in 1531 in a house at Carrer Rectoría 5, behind the church, which is now a shrine. There is another, smaller shrine with a fountain and ferns in Carrer de la Beatà, a quiet corner where caged birds sing. Almost every house has a tiled picture outside, depicting scenes from the saint's life and asking her blessing: 'Santa Catalina Tomás Pregau Per Nosaltres'. She was a farmer's daughter, marked out as special when still a child, and taken to Palma by a sympathetic patron, where she worked as a servant in a wealthy household before entering the convent of Santa Magdalena and taking her vows.

in the winter of 1838–39, of French writer George Sand – Armandine Dupin-Dudevant – and her lover, Frédéric Chopin, that really put the town on the map. They don't seem to have been very happy here; Chopin was unwell, the weather was miserable, and the villagers disapproved of Sand's habit of wearing men's clothes and smoking cigars. She disparaged the local people in her book, *A Winter in Majorca*, calling them 'barbarians and thieves', although she thought Mallorca 'the most beautiful place I have ever lived'.

Nowadays, coach loads of visitors disturb the peace of the little hilltop town as they come to see the couple's lodgings in the former Carthusian monastery, **La Real Cartuja de Valldemossa** (open Mar–Oct: Mon–Sat 9.30am–6pm, Sun 10am–1pm; Nov–Feb: 9.30am–4.30pm; entrance fee). The monastery was founded in 1399, but when the monks were expelled in 1835 some of their cells were sold as apartments

Valldemossa, crowned by the former monastery, is a fairytale town

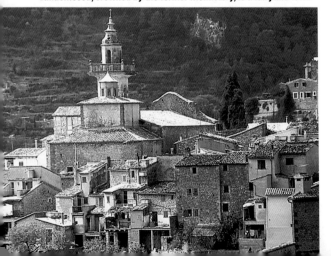

– although the 'cells' were three-room suites with private gardens. Those rented by Sand and Chopin are now a museum, which displays manuscripts, Chopin's death mask and his piano. You can also visit the massive church, the pharmacy, with a beautiful collection of 18th-century ceramic jars, the library and the Prior's Cell, complete with a life-size model of a prior. There is a **Museu Municipal** here, too, with documents relating to the Archduke Ludwig *(see page 48)*; and an **art gallery** displaying paintings by Joan Miró, Max Ernst and Antoni Saura as well as Mallorcan landscapes.

The adjoining 16th-century palace, the **Palau del Rei Sanxo** (hours as for La Cartuja; combined ticket), was constructed on the site of one Jaume II built for his son, Sanxo, and is entered through a tranquil, plant-filled courtyard. Piano recitals of Chopin's music are held throughout the day.

Around the Town

Outside the monastery is a cobbled *plaça* shaded with lime trees – *tilos* – which give the square its name. The streets around it, and those leading to the 13th-century church of Sant Bartomeu, dedicated to Santa Catalina, are bright with potted plants, and the steepest, most slippery parts are covered with strips of carpet to prevent trippers tripping up.

The main street in the lower town, where there are adequate car parks, is lined with cafés and restaurants and some interesting little shops, selling jewellery and clothes made of cool, natural fibres. One of the nicest bars (just back from the main street, on Carrer Blanquera) serves delicious *horchata (see page 101),* fresh juice and good coffee and hot chocolate, along with *cocas de patata*, the sugar-dusted, potato-shaped buns, tasting not unlike *ensaimadas*, that are a local speciality.

On the edge of town, going towards Palma, is the **Centro Cultural Costa Nord** (open daily 9am–6pm; tel: 971 612

Na Foradada is at its most magical at sunset

425 for details), founded by Michael Douglas, who has had a home nearby for many years, and who narrates the commentary to a virtual reality tour of the region.

In the other direction, a few metres along the road towards Banyalbufar, a vertiginous road leads 6km (4 miles) down to the tiny **Port de Valldemossa** where there's a small gravel beach and crystal-clear water. On summer weekends, however, the narrow road and the limited parking area become uncomfortably busy.

Son Marroig

The coastal C710 continues north, with stunning sea views to the left, and groves of ancient, gnarled olive trees among huge boulders to the right. Just outside Deià, a sign points to **Son Marroig** (open Mon–Sat 9am–8pm; till sunset in winter; entrance fee), an 18th-century manor house that belonged to the Austrian Archduke Ludwig Salvator of Habsburg-Lorraine and Bourbon, who had a life-long love affair with the Balearics and their people. Born in Florence in 1847, he renounced courtly life in Vienna and spent years travelling the world on scientific explorations, returning often to the estate he bought in 1870 on this beautiful stretch of coast. There are several rooms that can be visited, filled with paintings, photos and ceramics. In the gardens, there's a wonderful view from a cliff-edge white temple, built of Carrara marble.

Hundreds of metres below the house is **Na Foradada**, a rocky promontory, pierced by a remarkable 18-m (60-ft) wide natural window. If you visit the house, ask for permission to make the half-hour walk down to the sea and the landing stage where the Archduke used to anchor his steam-driven yacht, *Nixe*. The café near the car park is a wonderful place from which to watch the sun set over the sea. (For details of concerts at Son Marroig as part of the Deià International Music Festival, *see page 93*.)

Deià

Set on the slopes of the 1,062-m (3,484-ft) Teix massif, **Deià**  is a delight, a pretty town of honey-coloured stone that has attracted artists, writers and assorted expatriates ever since the Archduke Ludwig first came here. He was followed by the Catalan poet and painter Santiago Rusinyol, at the turn of the 20th century, later by writer Anaïs Nin (1903–77) and the American archaeologist William Waldren. But it is Robert

The Teix massif forms a dramatic backdrop to pretty little Deià

Graves, the poet and author of *I, Claudius* and the autobiographical *Goodbye to All That*, who came here with American writer Laura Riding in 1929, who is most closely associated with the place. Graves loved Deià and fiercely defended the northwest coast against commercial exploitation. It was largely due to his efforts that the area was designated a protected zone.

You must leave your car on the main street, which is lined with restaurants, galleries and shops selling attractive summer clothes. Narrow, winding streets lead to the top of the village and the little church of **Sant Joan Bautista**, where taped sacred music plays. Beside it is a small cemetery overlooking the Mediterranean; a simple cement slab, on which there are usually fresh flowers or plants, bears the scrawled inscription 'Robert Graves, Poeta, 1895–1985'.

The town is extremely popular in summer, and house prices and rents are high because so many chic and well-heeled people have holiday homes here. Besides a luxury hotel, La Residencia, there are several less expensive alternatives, and the best selection of restaurants on the coast *(see pages 130 and 139)*.

Cala de Deià and Llucalcari

Just past the village, a twisting 2-km (1-mile) drive takes you down to Cala de Deià, a tiny cove with a rocky beach, where ramps emerge from boathouses set into the cliffs. The water is clear, buoyant and safe for children and there are two reasonable beach cafés. Don't imagine you've found a secluded beach, though. Regular visitors know it well and it can get very busy at weekends.

You can walk to the beach, too, either by following steps near the vehicle access road, or by walking down steep Carrer Bauza at the Valldemossa end of the village. You pass the

Boathouses in the cliffs at Cala de Deià

Deià Archaeology Museum and Research Centre (open Tues, Fri, Sun 5.30–7pm only; entrance fee), founded in the 1960s by Graves and William Waldren, with exhibitions of works by local artists and archaeological finds, then follow the course of a stream past pretty gardens till the village peters out and the path continues through groves of lemons and olives, with helpful signs telling you how long it takes – it's about 35 minutes in all.

Shortly after Deià (going towards Sóller) is **Llucalcari**. It isn't properly signposted; look for the sign that says simply 'Hotel' off to the left. There is one good and surprisingly reasonable hotel *(see page 131)* and a handful of stone houses, several of them fortified, with coats of arms emblazoned on the doors. If you're up to a hike down the hill you'll discover a rocky section of shoreline with pristine, transparent waters. The bus between Palma and Sóller stops at the top of the access road.

Sóller and its Port

From Deià, the coast road, lined with groves of oranges, lemons and almonds as well as olives, descends into the broad valley of Sóller. The scenery is lovely and the town of **Sóller** itself is a little gem, a busy, prosperous place that claims, like several others, to have been the birthplace of Columbus. It is full of well-preserved 18th- and 19th-century mansions, and the main square, **Plaça Sa Constitució**, with numerous cafés, is a good place to sit and absorb the town's character. Like the main street, the Gran Via, it has *Moderniste* (Catalan Art Nouveau) flourishes, a legacy of early 20th-century expansion. The church of **Sant Bartomeu** (open Mon–Thur 10.30am–1pm, 2.45–5.15pm, Fri–Sat 10.30am–1pm; free) is a huge building with a baroque interior and attractive stained-glass windows. Its *Moderniste* exterior, like that of the Banco Central Hispano on the opposite corner, was designed by a pupil of Antoni Gaudí.

The station at the top of the town is another splendid *Moderniste* building. You can make an old-fashioned journey on a little train that has been running from here to Palma and back on a narrow-gauge railway since 1912 (journey time about one hour). If you are catching the train from Palma to Sóller, avoid the Tren Turístic at 10.40am and 12.15pm. It's the same train making the same journey – except that it has one photo-stop en route – but the price is double that of the usual trip.

From outside the station, where the tourist office is

> **Sóller is a good place to try freshly squeezed orange juice (*zumo de naranja*), as the orange groves around the town are reputed to produce the very best juice oranges. It also has some tempting cake shops – try the thick, sticky fig cake or the *picos de marzapan*, little white triangular confections advertised as '*típico de Sóller*'.**

housed in an old wooden train carriage, you can catch the **Orange Tram** that rattles on a scenic, 20-minute journey to **Port de Sóller** (every half hour 7am–8.15pm), stopping en route where requested. There's a fine harbour here, and the slightly shabby beach is being tidied up. Despite some unattractive modern buildings, this is a good old-fashioned little resort, where you can hire canoes, take sailing or windsurfing lessons or make boat trips around the bay or further afield to Sa Calobra and Na Foradada (*see What to Do, page 83*).

The Orange Tram reaches the port

Two Gardens

Just outside Sóller, on the ring road, is the **Museu Balear de Ciències Naturals i Jardí Botànic de Sóller** (open Tues–Sat 10am–6pm, Sun 10am–2pm; entrance fee), which has an interesting collection of aromatic herbs and plants from all over the Balearic Islands.

The road from Sóller to Palma, with numerous hairpin bends and the 496-m (1,627-ft) **Coll de Sóller** pass to negotiate, was believed to be so daunting that it impeded the development of the area. Despite the protests of some environmentalists, a tunnel was constructed under the mountains, reducing travel time to Palma to about half an hour (toll €3.50).

At the southern exit from the tunnel are the **Jardins d'Alfàbia** (open Sept–May: Mon–Fri 9.30am–5.30pm, Sat 9.30am–1pm; Jun–Aug: 9.30am–6.30pm; entrance fee), a baronial mansion with wonderful gardens that was once the country estate of a Moorish *vizier* of Palma. The cisterns, fountains and irrigation channels are a bit neglected, but the flowing water and shaded walks, with turkeys pecking under fig trees, and birds singing among exotic plants, are appealing. The house is full of treasures: look out for the huge, 14th-century oak chair in the print room, regarded as the most important antique in Mallorca.

From Bunyola to the Castle

A few kilometres past the gardens a left-hand turn points to **Bunyola**, a peaceful little place that produces excellent olive oil and a bright green herbal liqueur called Palo Tunel. The village church and the town hall both stand on the main square, Sa Plaça, which is shaded by leafy plane trees. It's a lovely drive from here to the tiny village of **Orient**, which has a hotel and several restaurants and is a favourite base for hikers. The **Castell d'Alaró**, a ruined fortress built by Jaume I, crowns a massive crag 822m (2,700ft) high.

You can walk up from Orient if you have plenty of energy, strong shoes and a supply of drinking water, or drive most of the way to the summit up narrow, tortuous lanes, starting a little north of nearby **Alaró**. The tracks get progressively rougher, however, and the final stretch is only suitable for four-wheel-drive vehicles. Park before this section begins, at the Bar Es Pouet, and look for a sign saying 'Castell a Peu' (To the castle on foot). There's still a vigorous 30- to 40-minute climb to do, not advisable in the heat of summer. The views from the top are spectacular. There is a small restaurant and simple accommodation, which must be booked in advance (tel: 971 510 480).

Fornalutx – so pretty it's been designated a national monument

The Heart of the Tramuntana

If you go in the opposite direction from Sóller, towards Pollença, there are more magnificent views as the road cuts through the heart of the Serra de Tramuntana, over the pass of **Puig Major**, Mallorca's highest mountain at 1,445m/4,741ft.

Fornalutx is an exquisite little town of warm stone buildings that has been designated a national monument – which naturally means that it draws in a lot of visitors, but also means building regulations are stringent. Set against the backdrop of the Tramuntana range, its steep cobbled streets are lined with cacti and palm trees. A high number of the well-restored medieval properties belong to foreigners, attracted by the region's beauty. The town is set among ancient terraces of citrus fruits and gnarled olive trees, marked out with dry-stone walls. Paths run through them to pretty little **Biniaraix**, which is also only a half-hour walk down narrow lanes, signposted from the centre of Sóller.

A short distance past Fornalutx on the C710, the **Mirador de Ses Barques** has a restaurant where you can stop for a drink while enjoying views of the coast and Port de Sóller. The route then winds past the reservoirs of Panta de Cúber and Panta de Gorg-Blau, connected by a narrow canal. Near the latter, a little road leads down to the coast. Its name, **Sa Calobra** (The Snake), is an apt one for the 12km (8 miles) of hairpin bends that loop down to sea level. The views are stunning and the road is an adventure in itself, but try to come fairly early in the morning to avoid the streams of tourist coaches.

Park where you can when the road reaches sea level and walk a short distance towards the deep gorge of **Torrent de Pareis**. Tunnels burrow through the rock to the riverbed where the gorge widens into a huge natural theatre. The idyllic little bay, **Cala de Sa Calobra**, has a couple of restaurants and bars and a pebbly beach, but they all get crowded in summer.

Cala de Sa Calobra is idyllic – especially if you go by boat

The Monestir de Lluc

About 10km (6 miles) further along the road to Pollença, the **Monestir de Lluc** (open April–Sept: daily 10am–6.30pm; Oct–Mar: 10am–5.30pm) is the major pilgrimage site in Mallorca. Tucked in a valley near Puig des Castellot, the massive building dates mainly from the 18th century, but pilgrims have been coming here since the 13th century to pray to a dark-stone statue of the Madonna and Child, La Moreneta. According to legend, it

The Monestir de Lluc attracts tourists and pilgrims

was discovered by an Arab boy called Lluc, whose family had converted to Christianity. He took the statue to the church of Sant Pere in the tiny village of Escorça nearby, but it kept returning to the place where he had found it, so it was finally allowed to stay and a chapel was built to house it.

People still come to venerate La Moreneta, but many also come to have lunch and admire the views, for the monastery has a restaurant, bar and barbecue area. It also offers inexpensive accommodation (tel: 971 871 525/971 517 025) and although the rooms are fairly basic, staying in one of them allows you to appreciate the peace of the monastery and its surroundings after all the tour groups have gone home.

Attend Mass in the church (daily 11.15am) for the lovely experience of hearing the Lluc boys' choir, the **Coro Blavets** (The Blue Ones), named after the colour of their cassocks.

THE NORTH AND NORTHEAST

The north is a region of great variety. It encompasses the rugged Cap de Formentor, the sandy coves of Sant Vicenç, two attractive towns – Pollença and Alcúdia – the resort of Port de Pollença and the huge, curved Badia d'Alcúdia, lined with resorts and facilities. Parallel to the bay is a complete contrast in the wetlands of the Parc Natural de S'Albufera

From Palma, it's a fast drive up the main C713/PM220 to Pollença (around 50km/30 miles). If you are continuing the previous route, the road from Lluc curves through forests of holm oaks before descending to the gentle Vall de Son Marc and the town of Pollença.

Pollença

Pollença has a long history. The Romans established a settlement here after they moved inland from Alcúdia/Pollentia *(see page 64),* and the stone bridge to the north of the town

---

Puig de Santa Maria

Just outside Pollença on the Palma road is a path up to the **Santuari del Puig**, the ruined convent on 333-m (1,092-ft) **Puig de Santa Maria**. The first half of the 4-km (2-mile) trail can be done by car, the latter part on foot. The dry-stone walls *(margers)* along the last section are a good demonstration of an ancient skill that is now dying out. The views from the top, stretching as far as the Serra de Tramuntana, Cap de Formentor, the plain of Sa Pobla and the bays of Alcúdia and Pollença, are superb. The Gothic convent was founded in the 14th century and soon became one of the most sacred buildings on the island. Accommodation is available and there are self-catering facilities, a bar and a restaurant (prior notice needed for accommodation, tel: 971 184 132).

centre is Roman in origin. The Catalan community was founded in 1236 after the Moors were expelled from the island. Present-day Pollença was first shown on a map in 1789; it was a prosperous town, the property of the Order of the Knights of St John until 1802, and able to support the numerous impressive churches still standing – although some are now deconsecrated.

The cockerel on the fountain is a symbol of Pollença

Pollença is a lively place, especially on summer evenings when it fills with visitors; the comings and goings in the **Plaça Major** provide free entertainment for people sipping cool drinks outside one of the many cafés and restaurants. The *plaça* also comes into its own on Sunday morning, when local people shop for fresh produce in the market, then drink coffee outside the Café Espanyol after attending Mass in the parochial church, **La Mare de Déu des Àngels** (open Mar–Oct: Mon–Fri 11am–1pm; May–Jun and Sept–Oct: 3–5pm; free). There's a modern art gallery in the square, too: Galería Bennassar (open Mon–Sat 10am–1pm, 5–8.30pm, Sun 10am–1.30pm; entrance fee).

The Carrer de Monte-Sion leading off the square towards the Jesuit-founded church of the same name (not open to the public), has some great little shops and a number of restaurants. Good ceramics can be found in Monte-Sion Cerámica, which has a display of old decorated tiles – unfortunately not for sale. Nearby is little Plazuela de la Almoina; the central fountain has a cockerel on top, the symbol of the town.

From the parish church in the *plaça* (or from the Ajuntament, off to the left), the **Via Crucis** (Way of the Cross), a flight of 365 steps lined with cypress trees, leads to **El Calvari**. This little chapel has been given a rhyming name – **La Mare de Déu del Peu de la Creu** (Mother of God at the Foot of the Cross) – after a 14th-century sculpture inside showing Mary at the feet of Christ.

Back in town, the deconsecrated Dominican convent and church of **Sant Domingo** (church, cloister and museum open Tues–Sat 10.30am–1pm, 5.30–midnight; Sun 10.30am–1.30pm; entrance fee for museum) is now devoted to culture rather than worship. Exhibitions of installation art are staged in the nave of the great 17th-century church in summer, and the cloisters are the venue for a classical music festival in July and August *(see page 93)*, when an international line up of orchestras and soloists performs. Pollença's **Museu Municipal** is also housed inside the monastery in a large, light space. Somewhat eclectic, it includes changing exhibitions of contemporary paintings and sculpture, a permanent collection of Gothic art, some early 20th-century paintings by a local artist and a few archaeological finds.

Pollença's Via Crucis

Outside the convent, the **Jardins Joan March Severa**, built around a square watchtower, have an interesting collection of Balearic plants. Carrer Roser Vell leads off to the left; at its far end you'll see the plain façade of the little oratory of **Roser Vell** (open Apr–Oct: Mon–Fri 5–7pm; Nov–Mar: 3–5pm; free), begun early in the 14th century.

Boats moored in Port de Pollença

Cala Sant Vicenç and Port de Pollença

About 3km (2 miles) along the PM220 from Pollença to its port is the turning to **Cala Sant Vicenç**, a glossy resort built around three gorgeous sandy coves with brilliant blue water, excellent for swimming and snorkelling – although strong winds can get up quite quickly. The setting, framed by the craggy Serra de Comayaques and El Morral mountains, is spectacular; try to ignore the modern hotel on the headland.

A couple more kilometres along the main road brings you to **Port de Pollença**. Set on the wide curve of a bay, with the marina in the centre, it has been popular with English visitors for many years and retains a distinctive atmosphere. However, it is a resort with a split personality. To the north of the marina the promenade has a plethora of restaurants, some with tables set right on the beach, and a couple of stylish hotels. These give way to attractive, old, one-storey houses and wooden jetties, where the branches of pine trees almost reach the water.

On the promenade north of the marina you may notice a memorial bust of Hermen Anglada Camarasa (1872–1959), the Catalan *Moderniste* painter after whom this stretch is named. He lived and worked in Pollença for many years. A collection of his work can be seen in the Gran Hotel in Palma (*see pages 33–4*).

To the south of the marina, however, the palm-shaded promenade that parallels the lovely, long sweep of sandy beach is lined wall-to-wall with cheap and cheerful tripper shops and fast-food joints. The narrow streets behind the promenade are nicer. There's a lot to do, however: sailing and scuba lessons are on offer, and there are boat trips to Formentor and Cala Sant Vicenç.

Cap de Formentor

Continuing round the bay to the southeast, towards Alcúdia, the commercial zone ends abruptly and the beach becomes a narrow strip, popular with windsurfers, with an expanse of lonely wetlands on the other side.

But before heading in this direction, make a trip to the island's northernmost point, **Cap de Formentor**, the narrow headland on the north side of the Badia de Pollença. With sheer cliffs and idyllic sandy beaches, the rocky peninsula, surrounded by clear turquoise waters, is simply spectacular. The best place to appreciate the extraordinary landscape is the **Mirador des Colomer**, about 5km (3 miles) from Port de Pollença, where there is a specially designed walkway with telescopes. Some tour buses don't go any further than this, which is a blessing for motorists, as the twisting road is a challenging one, demanding much concentration, and can get swamped with traffic in summer.

The pretty, pine-shaded beach (signposted Platja de Formentor on the right-hand side), is a favourite spot for a picnic and offers splendid views across the bay – similar to those you would get from the exclusive Hotel Formentor, whose manicured gardens are visible from the beach. The hotel was built in 1928 by an Argentinian architect, Adam Diehl, and quickly became popular with a fashionable set which, over the next few decades, included the Duke of Windsor and Mrs Simpson, Sir Winston Churchill and the Rainiers of Monaco, and is still the haunt of the rich and famous.

From the beach turn-off it's about another 12km (8 miles) to the lighthouse on the tip. Just before you enter the tunnel that leads through the Fumat mountain, there's a great view of the sparkling waters of **Cala Figuera** far below, one of the most unspoilt beaches on the island. You may prefer to turn off down the single-track path to the tiny cove rather than continuing to the lighthouse. If you do carry on to the end, you'll find that the tiny car park can get crowded.

Appreciating the rugged cape scenery at Mirador des Colomer

Alcúdia

Retrace your steps now past Port de Pollença to the ancient, walled town of **Alcúdia**. There were Phoenician and Greek settlements here before the Romans founded their city in 123BC, and called it Pollentia (Power). They stayed for about five centuries before moving inland to present-day Pollença. The Vandals sacked it, the Moors rebuilt it – Al Kudia (means 'on the hill') – and the conquering Spaniards fortified it in the 13th century. The massive walls and gates now standing are later imitations, but still impressive. Today, it's a nice, unpretentious little place, with some excellent Renaissance façades, good cafés and restaurants on the central **Plaça Constitució**, and a lively Sunday market, held just outside the walls.

The sturdy Gothic church of **Sant Jaume** and adjoining **Museu Parroquial** (open Tues–Fri 10am–1pm, Sun 10am–

Posing with the giants outside Alcúdia's town hall

noon; entrance fee) form the southern bastion in the walls. Opposite the church, in a small, 14th-century building, the **Museo Monogràfic de Pollentia** (open Tues–Fri 10am–1.15pm, 3.30–5.15pm, Sat–Sun 10.30am– 12.45pm; combined entrance fee with Ciutat Romana, but either can be visited independently) has an extensive collection of Roman finds, including cera-

Market day in Alcúdia

mics, glassware, tools and surgical instruments. You can pick up a free leaflet here describing points of interest in the Roman city.

The remains of that city, the **Ciutat Romana del Pollentia** (open Tues–Fri 10am–3.30pm, Sat–Sun 10.30am–1.30pm; entrance fee), excavated in the 1950s by members of a dig organised by American archaeologist, William Bryant, stand outside the walls, on the road to the port (a bus from Palma stops nearby). The area includes remnants of two buildings, and gives an idea of the town's layout. The **Teatre Romà**, outside the city proper, is impressive and the acoustics (tested by many visitors) are great.

Port d'Alcúdia and the Bay

Port d'Alcúdia (from where you can get a ferry to Menorca) has evolved from a small fishing harbour into an all-purpose port for commercial, naval and pleasure craft and the largest resort on the north coast. Restaurants, cafés and discos have multiplied rapidly, as have high-rise hotels and apartment blocks, which now spread around the bay to form an almost unbroken ribbon of buildings 10km (6 miles) long.

Cattle graze in the wetlands of Parc Natural de S'Albufera

The stretch of glorious white sand beaches along the **Badia d'Alcúdia** in summer is a mass of bodies soaking up the sun or sheltering under colourful umbrellas. Although big, crowded and impersonal, the resort, which more or less merges into Can Picafort at the eastern end, does not have the seediness of some of the southern spots. Both remain pretty low-key, if a bit soulless, and are a good option for families with children or teenagers in need of entertainment.

As you drive along the main road, lined with supermarkets, shops and high-rise hotels, signs saying simply 'Platja' lead to the beach. Buses pick up passengers from hotels, and the little Moro Express road train covers some of the distance. The area around **Platja de Moro** is a bit quieter, but it is only just after sprawling **Can Picafort** that development ends, because the sands run out and the shore becomes rocky.

Parc Natural de S'Albufera

About halfway between Port d'Alcúdia and Can Picafort is the entrance to the **Parc Natural de S'Albufera** (open Apr–Sept: daily 9am–6pm; Oct–Mar: 9am–5pm; free). There's a not very clearly marked car park a few metres further along. It seems remarkable to find this huge area of precious wetlands so close to major resorts and it can be a real haven for visitors as well as for birds, more than 200 species of which have been spotted here. A free visitors' permit must be picked up from the helpful Reception Centre, about 1 km

(½ mile) from the entrance. The reserve covers 800 hectares (2,000 acres), with marked walking and cycling tracks through it, and is criss-crossed by a network of canals constructed in the 19th century by a British company that began reclaiming marshland for agriculture, but ran out of money. The area became a protected zone in 1988, one of the first beneficiaries of the new environmental consciousness in Mallorca.

THE CENTRAL PLAIN

The centre of Mallorca is called **Es Pla** (The Plain). Lightly populated, it is little geared towards visitors and doesn't receive many, but it shouldn't be neglected. There are lovely agricultural landscapes with ancient stone farmhouses, olive groves and unassuming old towns. It is known as 'the land of a thousand windmills' and while it's unlikely that anyone has counted, there certainly are a lot of them. They are a characteristic of the island, and many have been restored and put back into use, particularly around Sa Pobla.

Just one of Mallorca's 'thousand windmills'

This route starts from Pollença and visits several of the inland towns, with a detour to Randa, the 'monastery mountain', but narrow country roads run off in all directions and are worth exploring.

Sa Pobla

The PM220 runs about 12km (8 miles) through fertile farmland to **Sa Pobla**, an unexceptional but pleasant town with several fine old buildings around the main square and a church consecrated to Sant Antoni Abat. A reputable jazz festival takes place in Sa Pobla throughout August.

> On 16 January a popular festival in honour of Sant Antoni Abat is celebrated in Sa Pobla, with bonfires and music and the eating of *espinagades* (pastries filled with spiced vegetables and S'Albufera eel). The next day, the town's pets are led in a procession through the streets and blessed outside the church.

From here you can continue down the main C713 to **Inca**. It is not a particularly interesting town, but it is worth a visit for its *cellers (see panel on page 70)* and for the factory shop selling Camper shoes *(see page 90)*.

Binissalem and Sineu

Binissalem is about 8km (5 miles) further down the main road, in the heart of the wine-producing district. You will see vineyards stretching for miles around – particularly attractive in late summer, when grapes are nearly ready for picking. There's a wine festival here at the end of September.

It's nicer, though, to take the rural (but good) road to **Sineu**, at the centre of the island, the pick of the inland towns. It has an elegant Gothic church, with some lovely reliefs by the Mannerist Gaspar Gener (1563–90), a baroque retable and some interesting modern stained glass. There are also some attractive baronial homes in the town, and a peaceful plaza with good restaurants. On the outskirts of town, the **Centre d'Art S'Estació** (open Mon–Fri 9.30am–1pm, 4–7pm, Sat 9.30am–1pm; free) stages exhibitions of contemporary art in a disused station building.

In Costitx, situated just 7km (4 miles) to the west of Sineu, the **Planetarium** (open Mon–Fri 10am–2pm, 4–6pm; entrance fee) is both entertaining and educational.

From Petra to the Sanctuaries

From Sineu it's about 11km (6 miles) to **Petra**. As you enter the town, you will see, on your right, the brand new **Ca N'Oms** (open Mon–Sat 11am–1pm, 6–10pm; free), a modern art gallery with sculpture in a pleasant

Modern art in Sineu's Centre d'Art S'Estació

garden, and a smart, minimalist bar (closed at lunchtime).

The main reason people go to sleepy little Petra is to visit the **Casa Museu Fray Juníper Serra** (opening times vary; a notice outside tells you where to get the key; donation requested). Petra is the birthplace of Fray Serra (1713–84), one of Mallorca's best-known sons, a Franciscan monk who founded numerous missions in California. The museum, run by a dedicated Society of Friends, illustrates these and other New World missions; his house next door is more interesting, a modest place with cell-like rooms and a pretty garden.

Ask at the museum if it is possible to visit the monastery of Sant Bernardino, opposite, where wall tiles depict the Californian missions and signs lead to Es Celler (*see box on page 70*).

From Petra it is less than 5km (3 miles) to the main Palma road (C715). The first town en route in the direction of Palma is Vilafranca de Bonany, known for the production of sweet little tomatoes, garlic, red peppers and melons. A little further along, a turning on the right takes you to **Els Calderers de Sant Joan** (open Apr–Oct: daily 10am–6pm; Nov–Mar: 10am–5pm; entrance fee), a splendid 18th-century manor house with a chapel, a granary and an extensive estate and farm. You can sample homemade products as part of a tour.

Still heading towards Palma, turn off at Algaida to visit 542-m (1,778-ft) **Puig de Randa**, the highest point on the plain, crowned by the **Santuari de Nostra Senyora de Cura** (accommodation available; tel: 971 120 260). The original sanctuary here was established by the mystic, Ramón Llull (1235–1316). On your way up you pass the Oratori de Gràcia and the hermitage of Sant Honorat. Randa is the centre of a little cluster of sanctuaries. Not far away, the Ermita de la Pau has a Romanesque chapel; and just above the village of Porreres you can drive the 4km (2½ miles) up to the **Santuari de Montesió**, which contains a 15th-century marble statue of the Verge de Montesió. There is a bar, restaurant, and accommodation (tel: 971 647 185).

To return to Palma, take the C717 or C715. For the east coast, take the C715 towards Manacor, then north to Artà.

Cellers

Anyone interested in the true *cuina Mallorquina* – Mallorcan cooking – should visit a *celler*. These cool basement *bodegas* were originally wine shops and are still lined with huge oak barrels, but have now become restaurants, serving large helpings of island food. They exist all over the island, but there are some especially renowned ones in the inland towns. Inca has about half a dozen, of which Can Amer is the best known. In Sineu, the Ca'n Font on the main square is the place to go, while Petra's best is Es Celler (see page 142 for details). They won't suit anyone who wants to eat outside in the sun, but their cavernous depths can be refreshing on a hot day.

Platja Canyamel on the southeast coast

THE EAST AND SOUTHEAST

The bays and beaches along the east coast have become somewhat overdeveloped and overcrowded, but the resorts are nicer and far less excessive than those around the Bay of Palma, and some spots – harbours such as Port Colom and Cala Figuera – are delightful. There are also two fortified towns in the northeast corner – Artà and Capdepera – and several amazing caves to visit, plus the Bronze Age sites of Ses Païsses (near Artà) and Capocorp Vell, near the south coast.

Artà and Ses Païsses

Artà lies about 12km (8 miles) inland, a fortified town that ◀ has retained a friendly, everyday atmosphere, and not become a mere showcase for its historic sites. It has a couple of good hotels with restaurants *(see pages 134–5)* and would make a pleasant place to stay if you feel like escaping the razzle-dazzle of the coast.

The great fortress at Artà, surrounded by battlements

In a palazzo on the Plaça d'Espanya, the **Museu Regional d'Artà** (open Mon–Fri 10am–1pm; entrance fee) stands next to the town hall and contains archaeological finds dating from Phoenician, Greek and Roman times, as well as a natural science collection.

The ancient church of the **Transfiguració del Senyor**, with a large rose window above the main portal, is one of Artà's major sites. Beyond, the Via Crucis (Way of the Cross), a broad flight of steps flanked by cypress trees and stone crosses, leads to the **Santuari de Sant Salvador d'Artà**. This great fortress, begun in the 13th century on the remains of a Moorish structure, is enclosed by a battlemented wall, along which you can walk for splendid views across the plain to the coast. You may be lucky and arrive when a recital is being given in the church – a wonderful experience.

The prehistoric settlement of **Ses Països** (open April–Sept: daily 9am–1pm, 3–7pm; Oct–Mar: Mon–Sat 9am–1pm, 2.30–5pm) is about 2 km (1 mile) from Artà on a track sign-posted simply 'Talayot'. A path leads from the well-shaded car park through an impressive gateway in the Cyclopean wall surrounding the settlement. The ruins – which are in need of a little love and attention – include several square foundations, a *talayot* (tower) with a small chamber at its base, and an oval room called a *naveta*, with the remains of several pillars.

Capdepera

Barely 8km (5 miles) east of Artà is the ochre-coloured town of **Capdepera**, its streets filled with flowers. Steps lead from the Plaça d'Espanya to the **Castell de Capdepera** (open Apr–Oct: daily 10am–8pm; Nov–Mar: 10am–5pm; entrance fee). The largest castle in Mallorca, it originated in Roman times, the Moors enlarged it and the Christians strengthened it further. Below the defensive wall, from which there is a superb view, stands the 19th-century church of Sant Bartomeu.

From Capdepera a road runs through farmland, past the Canyamel Golf Club, where a new road layout promises urbanisation to come, then winds high above the **Platja Canyamel** development to the **Coves d'Artà** (open Apr–Sept: daily 10am–7pm; Oct–Mar: 10am–5pm; frequent guided tours; entrance fee). Carved out of the sheer cliff face, the caves are less commercialised than the Coves del Drac *(see page 75)* and the limestone rock formations are quite awesome.

Cala Ratjada

It's only 3 km (2 miles) from Capdepera to **Cala Ratjada**, a busy resort built on a grid pattern. It used to be the most important fishing harbour on the island, after Palma, but much of its large port is now used for leisure and pleasure, as you can see from the boats moored here. There is plenty of accommodation, although a large percentage of it is pre-booked by German tour companies, and a rash of fast-food restaurants and tourist-tat shops detracts from the atmosphere. How-

There is a fast passenger ferry from Cala Ratjada to Ciutadella, Menorca, which takes just 75 minutes. There are some good day-return deals available; some include bus transport to Palma. If you are taking a car over, however, you must use the Alcúdia ferry *(see page 124 for details).*

ever, much of the seafront is attractive, with restaurant tables set among pines and succulents.

There is one sandy beach in the centre of town, where good waves attract surfboarders, but most people head through shady pines to the beaches a little further north. The northernmost one is **Cala Mesquida**, with beautiful, protected dunes and excellent surfing waves.

The **Platja de Son Moll** to the south of the resort can be reached via the beach promenade. Still further south is **Sa Font de Sa Cala**, named after a freshwater spring that flows directly into the sea. Here, a lovely little beach has been completely overwhelmed by two huge hotel complexes.

On a hill above Cala Ratjada's harbour, the **Jardins Casa March** can only be visited by appointment with the tourist office (tel: 971 563 033), but the impressive modern sculpture displayed there makes it worth the effort.

Cala Ratjada's harbour is mainly used for leisure boats these days

Cala Millor to Porto Cristo

The next resort complex, the largest and loudest on the east coast, is **Cala Millor**, where three separate *calas* merge together along the sandy beach of Son Severa. The resort is still growing, with new roads being laid and apartments constructed on the outskirts. The neighbouring promontory of **Punta de N'Amer**, a 200-hectare (495-acre) nature reserve, is the only area that hasn't been developed.

The road south passes the Safari-Zoo *(see page 88)* before reaching **Porto Cristo**, an old-fashioned resort with a pleasant, local atmosphere. There is a huge yacht marina, an unremarkable beach and a couple of traditional hotels vying with modern buildings. It's popular with Mallorcan visitors at weekends, and the narrow streets can get clogged.

Most of the tour buses here are ferrying visitors to the **Coves del Drac** (open Apr–Oct: daily 10am–5pm; Nov–Mar: 10.45am–3.30pm; entrance fee), south of the town. Several daily tours run through the brightly lit 2km (1 mile) of huge chambers and spectacular formations. The highlight is the 177-m (581-ft) long subterranean lake named after Edouard-Alfred Martel, the French speleologist who explored the caves in 1896. Jules Verne is said to have been inspired by a visit to write *Journey to the Centre of the Earth*.

Felanitx and the Santuari de Sant Salvador

It's a pleasant drive south through agricultural land, with minor roads leading off to beaches. To the right, just before Porto Colom, is **Felanitx** – you will see a series of watchtowers on the hill as you approach. This was the birthplace, in 1957, of the celebrated painter Miquel Barceló, and it is a good place to buy ceramics. There's a lively market on Sunday morning, and an impressive, partly 13th-century church, Sant Miquel.

En route to Felanitx, turn off to the **Santuari de Sant Salvador**, on a hill 509m (1,670ft) above sea level. The first

Far-reaching views from the Santuari de Sant Salvador

sanctuary here was built in 1348 and today's structure dates from 1734. On one side of the hill is a 14-m (46-ft) stone cross, and on the other the monument to Cristo Rei (both 20th century). The monastery church contains a fine alabaster retable showing scenes from the Last Supper (c. 1500). Strangely, there are also a number of jerseys belonging to a championship cyclist, which are fading in glass cases along with notes of homage to the virgin.

You can drive right up to the sanctuary and park. There is a bar and restaurant, a barbecue area and picnic site, some simple accommodation (tel: 971 827 282) and magnificent views over much of the island.

Porto Colom to Cala Mondragó

Reached on the PM401 from Felanitx, **Porto Colom** is still a working fishing port, where you can watch the catch brought ashore. There's a tiny strip of beach along the bay, en route to a lighthouse, but the lack of a significant, sandy beach has ensured that Porto Colom remains a pleasant place, with a pine-shaded promenade and some pretty, pastel-coloured houses. The only real development is around the bay at Cala Marsal to the south of the harbour.

Cala d'Or is only 7km (4 miles) further south, but you have to go inland then return to the coast. A resort of many years standing, it has evolved into a huge complex encompassing several different coves and beaches. The architecture is pretty homogeneous – low-rise, flat-roofed and snowy-white. The coves are pretty and the swimming is good, the harbour plays host to some elegant yachts, and there are all the tourist facilities and water sports you could hope for, as well as a plethora of bars and discos.

If you want to get away from it all, you must go a little further south to **Porto Petro**, an attractive harbour with a yacht club and some nice restaurants; then wend your way to **Cala Mondragó**, which is off the beaten track and practically undeveloped in comparison with most of the coast. It should stay that way, as the two pleasant little sandy beaches are part of the **Parc Natural Mondragó** (information office open daily 9am–4pm; free) which also encompasses farmland and wetlands. There are walking tracks through the park and lots of opportunities to bird watch and look for wild orchids growing beneath the trees. A couple of inexpensive hotels and beach restaurants are here but it's all very low key.

Santanyí and Cala Figuera

Return to the main road and after 5km (3 miles) you'll come to **Santanyí**, a mellow little town of honey-coloured sandstone with one gate, Sa Porta Murada, remaining from the fortified walls. The huge parish church of **Sant Andreu Apostel** dominates the elongated Plaça Major, where there are some friendly cafés. There's an arty feel to Santanyí, with several exhibition venues, and a number of antiques and ceramics shops.

Cala Figuera is delightful, a fishing port with neat green-and-white houses and a walkway alongside the boathouses

Specimens at Botanicactus

right at the water's edge. A handful of leisure boats bob in the waters, but they do not outnumber or outshine the working vessels. There are plenty of restaurants and some accommodation but the tourist industry has not got out of hand.

Botanicactus and Es Trenc

Back to the main road again, and the first stop after Santanyí is **Botanicactus** (open daily 9am–7.30pm; entrance fee). Covering 150,000 sq m (178,000 sq yd) it is said to be one of the best botanical gardens in Europe, and contains 1,500 different plant species. It's not all cacti – there's an artificial lake surrounded by palms, and a stunning assortment of indigenous flowers.

Some 7km (4 miles) from Botanicactus is **Colònia de Sant Jordi**. It's a rather nondescript little resort, but its harbour is the starting point for trips to Cabrera *(see panel)*. To the west of Sant Jordi the sandy stretch of **Platja Es Trenc** (popular for nude bathing) has become a protected area, so major development will not be permitted.

From Campos to Palma

The main road west from Santanyí goes to **Campos**, a friendly town with two huge, sandstone churches. The Església Parroquial contains a famous painting by Murillo (1617–82) but it is usually closed. Ask for the key at the Casa Rectoría near the church's side door in Carrer del Bisbe Talladas. On the other side of the main road stands the arcaded town hall, while the Banco de Santander occupies a splendid building opposite a brutally modernised square.

The road then heads to **Llucmajor**, an ancient town with a history of shoemaking and a few striking *Moderniste* buildings. Follow signs to **Capocorp Vell** (open Fri–Wed 10am–5pm), the best-known Bronze Age site in Mallorca. The foundations of 28 enormous buildings can be seen, and at the edge of the settlement there are two massive square *talayots* and three round towers.

You can drop down to **Cabo Blanc** now, where a light-house stands on a rocky promontory. From here the road runs along a fairly dull stretch of coastline towards the long expanse of the **Platja de Palma**. **S'Arenal**, the largest resort, merges into **Les Meravelles** on a 7-km (4-mile) strip of packed beaches, fast-food outlets, high-rise hotels, high-throttle discos, English pubs, Murphy's bars and German beer halls. By the time you reach the beach and yacht harbour of **Ca'n Pastilla**, you are almost back in the capital.

Cabrera

Cabrera, a tiny, uninhabited island 17km (10 miles) to the south of Cap de Ses Salines, has been a nature reserve since 1991 (boat trips daily from April to October; tel: 971 649 034). It's just 7km (4 miles) by 5km (3 miles) in extent with a rocky coast and rugged limestone centre where a track leads 72m (236ft) up to the castle. There are two little bays, good for swimming and snorkelling. Bring your own supplies because there is nowhere to buy food or water or eat out. During the Napoleonic Wars, Cabrera was used to house French prisoners, and in Franco's time Spanish soldiers were quartered here.

WHAT TO DO

SPORTS

Most outdoor activities in Mallorca revolve around the water and there is a great range of things to do, including sailing, windsurfing, kitesurfing, paragliding, water-skiing, snorkelling, fishing and, of course, swimming. However, walking, climbing and bird watching are catching up in popularity, drawing thousands of visitors to the island, especially in spring and autumn, when the mild weather makes walking a pleasure, and numerous species of migrating birds delight birdwatchers. Mallorca is also a great place for cycling, horse riding and golf.

Sailing

The Balearics are a sailing paradise. Among those who recognise this are King Juan Carlos, who sails the royal yacht around the coast every summer; and Michael Douglas, who is one of those backing Palma's bid to hold the Americas Cup in 2007. The island has a wealth of safe harbours and some 40 marinas, and thousands of foreign visitors keep their own boats here all year round.

You can **hire** various kinds of craft for an hour, day or week at many beaches and hotels (but you must produce proof of qualification for a self-drive motor boat). The **Asociación Provincial de Empresarios de Actividades Marítimas de Baleares** (APEAM) is the biggest yacht charter company; for information, visit <www.apeam.com>. The **Centro Náutico Port de Sóller**, Platja d'En Repic, Port de Sóller, tel: 971 633 001, <www.nauticsoller.com>, is also recommended. For **sailing lessons**, the **Escuela Nacional de**

Windsurfers have a wonderful time in Mallorca

Vela Calanova, Avinguda Joan Miró 327, Palma, tel: 971
402 512, offers intensive beginners' courses and general advice, as does the **Centro Náutico Port de Sóller** *(see previous page)*. **Sail and Surf Pollença**, Passeig Saralegui, Port de
Pollença, tel: 971 865 346, is a prestigious sailing club that
offers instruction for beginners and more advanced sailors.

Windsurfing and Water-Skiing
There are windsurfing schools at several of the larger resorts
and you can also hire equipment. **Centro Náutico Port de
Sóller** and **Sail and Surf Pollença** *(see above)* both offer
windsurf hire and tuition, as does **Llaüts**, Camino San Carlos 6A, Port d'Andratx, tel: 971 672 094. In Sant Elm,
there's a water-ski school and hire outlet at **El Pescador**
restaurant at the end of the promenade (tel: 639 686 004). On
the east coast, windsurfing facilities are available at Cala
Millor and Cala d'Or.

Water-skiing equipment can be hired on many of the
major beaches, including Cala Millor, Can Picafort and Port
d'Alcúdia. The **Ski Club Calanova**, Carrer Condor 22, Son
Ferrer, Santa Ponça, tel: 971 100 328, is recommended.

Scuba Diving
Mallorca's crystal-clear waters, especially in the shallow
coves on the south and east coasts, are ideal for diving.
Scuba-diving equipment is for hire, if you have a qualification from your home country. The **Federación Balear de
Actividades Subacuaticas**, Polideportivo Son Moix, Camí
Vecinal de la Vileta 40, Palma, tel: 971 288 242, <www.
fbdas.com>, can give information and advice. The numerous
scuba diving clubs include **Aqua Marine Diving**, Port d'Andratx, tel: 971 674 376, and **Scuba Activa**, Sant Elm, tel: 971
239 102, in the southwestern corner; and **Mero Diving**, Cala
Ratjada, tel: 971 565 467, in the northeast.

Some fishing boat skippers may offer trips around their harbours

Boat Trips

From various points along the west coast, **Creuer-Sóller**, Muelle Comercial s/n, Port de Sóller, tel: 689 686 834, and its associate companies **Tramontana S.A**, tel: 971 633 109, and **Barcos Azules**, tel: 971 630 170, run a variety of trips around the rugged coast and tiny bays, including Cap Formentor and Sa Calobra. Boat trips operate from most ports; some use glass-bottomed boats, such as the **Dolphin D'Or**, tel: 971 657 012, which runs from Porto Colom. The tourist office produces a leaflet listing dozens of them, with contact details, but you will also see them advertised in the harbours.

Walking and Climbing

The Mallorcan landscape is perfect for dedicated hikers and more leisurely walkers. April and May, with a wild profusion of flowers, are the best months and September and October are good, too. In the hotter months, start early or make use of the long evenings. Needless to say, correct footwear is essential and common sense will tell you that a supply of water, a sunhat and sunscreen are wise precautions.

The **Serra de Tramontana** makes for the most dramatic scenery, especially on the climb to Castell d'Alaró *(see page 54)* and between the Monasteri de Lluc and the coast. In the southeast corner, there are numerous walking trails through the pine groves, marshlands and dunes of the **Parc Natural de Mondragó** (Information Centre open Mon–Fri 9am–4pm, tel: 971 181 022). These are on flatter terrain and more gentle than those in the northwest. The tourist office in Sóller, tel: 971 638 008, produces a leaflet outlining 20 walking excursions in the northwest of the island.

There are also serious rocks here for serious climbers. Contact the **Federación de Montañismo**, Carrer Pere d'Alcantara Penya 13, Palma, tel: 971 468 807, or **Grup Excursionista de Mallorca**, Carrer Andreu Feliu 20, Palma, tel: 971 947 900, <www.gemweb.org>. A useful private company is **Rocaroja**, Plaza del Mercat 15-1, Palma, tel: 616 754 679, e-mail: info@rocaroja.com, <www.rocaroja.com>. They can give advice on new routes and crags and those that are no longer accessible, and can also arrange all-in packages for climbers.

Climbing is becoming increasingly popular in Mallorca

Golf

There are twelve 18-hole golf courses on Mallorca, and all are challenging enough for even the best players. You can also hire equipment and take lessons. The beautifully landscaped **Son Vida Golf**, tel: 971 791 210, hosts the Balearics' Open, while the course at **Golf Santa Ponça**, tel: 971 690 211, is one of Europe's longest. On the east side of the island, **Canyamel**, tel: 971 564 457, and **Capdepera**, tel: 971 565 875, are both popular. For further information, contact the **Federació Balear de Golf**, Avinguda del Rei Jaume III 17, Palma, tel: 971 722 753.

There are walkers' maps available in La Casa de la Mapa, Carrer Sant Domingo 13, Palma and the bookshop of the Fundació La Caixa, Plaça Weyler 3, Palma, which also stocks a helpful book called *48 Walks in Mallorca* by Rolf Goetz (Rother Walking Guides; check <www.cordee.co.uk> for UK distributors). A number of excellent books on walking in Mallorca are also available in the UK from reputable bookshops.

Bird Watching

Mallorca is one of the most rewarding bird watching sites in Europe. The island's resident birds are enticing enough, but it's the visiting species that generate most excitement. Migrants stop off in spring – as many as 200 species have been spotted – and some stay for the summer. The most rewarding sites are the **Tramuntana** region, where rare black vultures and other birds of prey can be seen; the **Parc Natural de Mondragó**, tel: 971 181 022, for marine birds; and **Parc Natural de S'Albufera**, tel: 971 892 250, <mallorcaweb.net/salbufera>, for the widest variety of all.

Horse Riding

There are a number of small ranches and stables scattered all over the island and some *agroturisme* properties offer treks or can arrange them for you. A few of the reputable riding schools are: **Escuela de Equitación de Mallorca**, Carretera

Horse trekking is an agreeable way to see parts of the island

Sóller Km 12.2, tel: 971 613 157; **Rancho La Romana**, Peguera, tel: 971 687 084; and **Club Hípico San Jorge**, Rancho Veracruz, S'Arenal, tel: 971 402 023.

Cycling

In the spring, thousands of serious cyclists come to Mallorca from all over Europe to race over the island and grind up steep mountain passes. Summer tourists make more gentle progress on bikes they hire at the resorts. Check the brakes and tyres and make sure a strong lock and puncture kit is included. In Palma, **Rent a Bike Palma**, Carrer del Mar 10, tel: 971 718 158, will give details of the 30-km (18-mile) bike path that borders the Bay of Palma and suggest combined bike-and-train routes. Serious cyclists may want to contact the **Federación de Ciclismo**, Francesc Fiol i Juan 2, 1°, Palma, tel: 971 757 628.

Spectator Sports

Football is as popular in Mallorca as in other parts of Spain and there are dozens of clubs. The premier league team, **Real Mallorca**, plays at Son Moix stadium at Camí del Rei, Palma, e-mail: tickets@rcdmallorca.es.

Bullfights (*corridas*) exist, but they are not the big deal they are in some parts of the Spanish mainland. They're staged on summer Sunday afternoons in Palma's large Plaça de Toros. There are occasional bullfights in Alcúdia, Felanitx, Inca and Muro.

Horse races are held every Sunday, all year round, at the **Hipòdrom de Son Pardo** near Palma. The informal atmosphere and the casual-looking handicap starts can be deceptive, as competition is fierce. Betting is organised through a centralised tote system.

CHILDREN

Sandy beaches and calm, safe waters ensure that children can be happy on the beach for days at a time. But if that begins to pall, there are plenty of alternatives. The big resorts have a lot to offer in terms of entertainment such as water parks; they are quite expensive, but you can easily spend a whole day in them, which means you get your money's worth.

Not everything is black and white at the Safari-Zoo

Aquacity, Autovía Palma–Arenal Km 15, exit 13, tel: 971 440 000, at S'Arenal, with its mega-water slides, claims to be the biggest aquatic park in the world. **Aqualand Magaluf**, Carretera Cala Figuera, tel: 971 130 811, is another huge park, with a new attraction – the Boomerang slide. **Western Water Park**, Carretera Cala Figuera, Magaluf, tel: 971 131 203, has high-diving exhibitions, falcon displays and a cowboy show as added attractions. All open daily at 10am and there are special buses from the resorts.

In the north, **Hidropark**, Avinguda Tucán, Port d'Alcúdia, tel: 971 891 672, caters for younger children.

Marineland, Costa d'en Blanes, Calviá, Autovía Palma–Andratx, Portals Nous exit, tel: 971 675 125, has dolphins, sea lions, flamingos, toucans and performing parrots as well as a reptile house. Performing dolphins are a controversial subject, but at least the profits are ploughed back into conservation programmes.

For older children and teenagers, there is **Magaluf Karting**, Carretera Cala Figuera, tel: 971 131 134, next to the Aquapark. Older children may also appreciate **La Granja** *(see page 44)*, and the **Planetarium** *(see page 69)*, in Costitx. Kids of all ages love trips in the **Nemo Submarine**, which leaves from Magaluf, tel: 971 130 244 *(see page 40)*.

The **Safari-Zoo**, Carretera Porto Cristo–Cala Millor, tel: 971 810 909, on the east coast is usually a hit. The monkeys, antelopes, elephants, giraffes and rhinos can be observed from a mini-train, or from your own car.

The animals and the birds of prey – especially the demonstration sessions – at **La Reserva Puig de Galatzó** *(see page 44)* and **Natura Parc Santa Eugenia**, Carretera de Sineu Km 15, tel: 971 144 078, are other winners. And the vast model dinosaurs in the **Parc Prehistoric Son Gual** on the Carretera Palma–Manacor usually win approval.

Most children – apart from the very young – enjoy exploring caves. As well as the **Coves del Drac** at Porto Cristo *(see page 75)*, which are the most spectacular and best known, there are the **Coves d'Artà** at Canyamel *(see page 73)*, and the less visited **Coves dels Hams**, Carretera Porto Cristo–Manacor, tel: 971 820 988.

Museums aren't high on most kids' wish lists, but many of them – girls especially – enjoy the little dolls' museum, the **Museo de Muñecas Antiguas**, open Tues–Sun 10am–6pm, in Carrer Palau Real, on the approach to Palma's cathedral.

SHOPPING

Shopping in the Balearic Islands is more expensive than it used to be, but you will still find some excellent bargains, particularly if you are looking for leather goods or glass. If you're looking for designer labels, however, Carrer Verí, in Palma's old town, has some smart boutiques, as well as several antique shops. Avinguda Jaume III is the capital's major shopping street, lined with chic leather and clothing shops as well as department stores, including a huge branch of Spain's biggest, El Corte Inglés, which has a supermarket in the basement.

Lovely Leather

The Balearic Islands are justly famous for their leather industries. Excellent shoes, belts and bags and some of the

One of the chic little shops in Valldemossa

Mallorca's embroidered linen is a nice gift to take home

finest leather and suede jackets come from the islands. The focus of the leather industry in Mallorca is Inca, where you can shop at the factory outlets or the local market, which is fun, although the goods may not be any cheaper than you will find in Palma.

If you like shoes, you'll love shopping in Mallorca. You can go to the factory shop of the quirky shoe company **Camper** (look for signs on the main road), whose shoes are highly individual, some painted with flowers and trees, others with left and right partners slightly different. Camper also has an outlet in Palma, in Avinguda Jaume III. Less trendy, but extremely attractive and comfortable are *abarcas*, the slipper-like sandals made in Menorca that have been worn by peasants for centuries and have grown progressively less simple in recent years. You can still get the original versions in brown, black and neutral shades for around €20 and in a range of vivid and subtle colours for just a little more.

Linen

Mallorca's embroidered table and bed linens are quite attractive, and the market in Llucmajor is a great place to find them. Other towns known for good-quality embroidery are Manacor, Pollença and Artà. In Palma, you will see a number of shops selling fine, hand-embroidered linen – and a lot of others selling machine-made versions.

Glassware, Pottery and Pearls

High-quality **glassware** has been manufactured on the island for centuries. The **Gordiola Museu del Vidre** factory and museum, outside Algaida on the Palma to Manacor road, is a good place to go, as you can watch glass blowing and see some of the antique pieces on which many of the current products are based. They have a showroom in Palma, too, at Carrer Victoria 2.

Pottery is another traditional craft. There are two main types of cooking pots: *ollas* (round) and *greixeras* (flat and shallow). **Siurells** are small, clay figurines painted in red and green, based on Phoenician and Carthaginian originals.

Mallorcan cultured (artificial) **pearls**, Perlas Majorica, manufactured in Manacor, are exported in huge numbers. The best place to buy them is at the (well-signposted) **Pearl Centre** on the main road just outside the town, where you get a tour of the factory and have the biggest choice. You can buy them all over the island, however, including in Palma, at Avinguda Jaume III 11, and prices do not vary much from shop to shop. But don't imagine they are cheap because they are artificial.

Food and Drink

Mallorca is known for its herbal **liqueurs**, and the popular aperitif, **Palo Tunel**, made in Bunyola, is a novelty. Look for the bright green bottles with the train logo, on sale everywhere, and decide if you want the sweet variety *(dulce)* or the dry *(amargo)*. **Olive oil** from the same region is an excellent buy, not because it is cheap but because it is such good

Markets are held in towns all over the island

quality. **Olives**, too, are worth taking home. You can buy them in jars or tins, but to get a selection of true Mallorcan varieties, in all shapes, sizes and shades, acquire a plastic container and fill it up by selecting from the large tubs in the markets. For specialised foodstuffs the most fascinating place to shop is in the old-fashioned little **Colmado Santo Domingo** in Carrer Sant Domingo, near the city tourist office. You'll spot it immediately as it's festooned with hams, sausages and strings of peppers and garlic.

Markets

Weekly markets are held in small towns all over the island, where everything from fresh farm produce (including live chickens) to leather bags, household linen, pots and pans, sunglasses and sandals are for sale. They usually start fairly early in the morning and finish around 1pm. Particularly lively ones are held in Alcúdia on Tuesday and Sunday, in Pollença on Sunday and Sóller on Saturday. On Saturday morning in Palma the Baratillo, or flea market, is fun, even if you don't want to buy anything.

ENTERTAINMENT AND NIGHTLIFE

A monthly guide to events in Palma can be obtained from tourist offices and is found on <www.esinfotech.com/guia>. Otherwise there's the quarterly publication called *Events*, and listings in the *Mallorca Daily Bulletin*.

Palma has a lively classical music scene and there are two acoustically excellent concert halls, the Sala Magna and the Sala Mozart, in **L'Auditorio**, Passeig Marítim 18, tel: 902 332 211 for bookings, <www.auditorium-pm.com>. The Ciutat de Palma Symphony Orchestra has its home here and there's a varied programme of orchestral music, ballet, jazz and opera. Concerts are also held in the **Centro Cultural de la Misericòrdia** in Via Roma, tel: 971 713 346, and, in summer, in the delightful music room of the **Palau March**, tel: 971 711 122, <www.fundbmarch.es>. The grand Teatre Principal is currently closed for extensive renovation work, but the **Teatre Municipal**, Passeig de Mallorca 9, tel: 971 739 148, stages contemporary drama, dance and films. Free outdoor concerts – jazz, rock and classical – are held in the beautiful setting of the **Parc de la Mar** below the city walls on some summer evenings. A bar serves drinks and snacks and there's a cheerful party atmosphere.

Music Festivals

Summer is the time for music festivals, most of which are held in beautiful historic buildings. The best known is the Deià International Music Festival. Some performances are held in the parish church but most are in the stunning setting of Son Marroig (tel: 971 639 178 or e-mail patrickmeadows@wannadoo.es). The Chopin Festival has been held since 1980 in the cloister of La Cartuja in Valldemossa (tel: 971 612 351); and the Festival de Pollença (tel: 971 535 077; <www.festivalpollenca.org>) attracts international musicians to the lovely cloister of Sant Domingo. There is also a summer music festival with performances on various dates in Palma's Castell de Bellver (tel: 971 728 841) and in the Jardins Fundació March in Cala Ratjada (tel: 971 563 033). Sa Pobla hosts a good international jazz festival in August (tel: 971 542 530).

The Abaco bar is a novelty that's well worth a visit

Late Night Line-up

The bars, clubs and discos in the big resorts thump with loud music all night long and would be hard to miss. Needless to say, they rise and fall in favour, and predicting next season's hottest spot would be unwise. They are mostly geared to the teen and early-twenties age groups and there is no shortage of leaflets and posters trying to tempt customers.

Otherwise, most of Mallorca's nightlife is to be found in Palma, where the best clubs (currently) are **Pacha**, which has a split-level terrace and top DJs; and **Tito's**, which is popular with those who want to dance till dawn. Both are on the Passeig Marítim. The **Art Deco** disco, housed beside an old windmill in the Plaça del Vapor also has its fans. Remember that the action doesn't start until around midnight.

Outside the clubs, much of Palma's nightlife takes place in late-night bars, many of them in the Sa Llotja area, where most of the restaurants are. The kitsch **Abaco**, Carrer Sant Joan (off Apuntadors), tel: 971 71 59 74, with its exotic decor, caged birds, operatic background music and expensive cocktails, is an experience.

The **Atlántico**, Carrer San Feliu 12, is also popular for cocktails, but with rock instead of opera. **Café Barcelona Jazz Club**, Carrer Apuntadors 5, is a popular place that has been going for years, and plays a mixture of jazz, blues and Latin music; **Blues Ville**, Carrer des Moros 3 (also off Apuntadors), plays, as you would expect, blues. The **Yuppi Pub**, on Avinguda Joan Miró, is a popular gay music bar.

Calendar of Events

5–6 January: Three Kings (Reyes Magos) Procession in Palma.

16–17 January: Sant Antoni Abat festival in Palma, Artà, Sa Pobla and Manacor; animals are led in procession to be blessed by the patron saint of pets.

19–20 January: Sant Sebastià celebrated in Palma and Pollença, where the *cavallets* (small papier-mâché horses that the dancers strap round their hips) perform in a procession.

February: Carnival (Carnaval) celebrated in many towns and villages, with fancy dress parades and general revelry. This is a pre-Lent festival so dates vary depending on Easter.

March–April: Semana Santa (Holy Week) is celebrated in Palma and throughout the islands with solemn processions. In Pollença the Devallament (Lowering) sees a figure of Christ brought down from the Oratori on the hill.

8–10 May: Cristians i Morus festival, also called Ses Valentes Dones, in Sóller re-enacts a battle in 1561 when local women fought against invading Turkish pirates.

13 June: Sant Antoni de Padua festival in Artà. Lively festivities involve *cavallets* (*see above*) and fearsome black demons that cavort around the streets.

15–16 July: Día del Verge del Carmen, the patron saint of fishermen and sailors, is celebrated in many ports with processions on the water. Palma, Port de Sóller and Cala Ratjada are the principal venues.

last Sunday: Sant Jaume in Alcúdia is a big religious and secular festival.

24 August: Sant Bartomeu is celebrated in Capdepera and Montuïri with horse races and devil dancers.

28 August: Sant Agustí fiesta in Felanitx, with *cavallets* and *cabezudos* (big heads).

September – first Sunday: Processó de la Beatá in Santa Margalida.

last Sunday in September or first in October: the Festa des Butifarró in Sant Joan, with folk dancing and feasting on the famous Mallorcan black pudding (*butifarró*).

31 December: Festa de Standa in Palma commemorating the Christian reconquest of the island under Jaume I in 1229, with a procession.

EATING OUT

Restaurants in Mallorca cover a wide spectrum, from the excellent to the mediocre, from the local to the international. You will find traditional, rural cooking – the hearty *cuina mallorquina* – as well as ubiquitous Spanish dishes like paella and *gazpacho* that are very popular although they have little to do with the island. There has also been a recent emphasis on Basque cooking, which is regarded as one of the best regional cuisines in Spain; and there are refined dishes with a French flair in the more expensive restaurants. Several top-notch chefs are working on the island and, while a meal in one of their restaurants is not cheap, it is considerably less expensive than it would be in one of the European capitals. At the other end of the market there are, of course, such staples as chicken and chips, pizza, bratwürst and sauerkraut for people who like to stick with what they know. The list of recommended restaurants on *page 137* will help you make some informed choices.

Cuina Mallorquina

Much of the best cooking derives from simple, country fare, cooked in olive oil and made from whatever fresh ingredients are in season. *Cuina mallorquina* reaches its height in *cellers (see page 70)* but can be found in many other places, too. A meal usually starts with a dish of multi-coloured, oddly-shaped and quite delicious olives and a basket of rough-textured bread being brought to the table. There is sometimes a small charge for this, sometimes it is on the house.

Sopas mallorquinas – invariably referred to in this plural form – is a combination of vegetables, olives, garlic and sometimes pork. It is more like stew than soup, and makes a substantial first course. The *sopas* are usually served in an

Trying local dishes at lunchtime in Palma's restaurant district

earthenware bowl, or *greixera de terra,* which in turn gives its name to a complete range of casseroles: *greixonera de peix,* is a fish stew, and *greixonera d'alberginies* (or *berenjenas* in Castilian) is a wonderful aubergine concoction.

Another speciality is *tumbet*, a dish of peppers, aubergines, tomatoes and potatoes, coated in beaten egg and baked in the oven. This often features as a first course, but can be very filling so should be followed by something fairly light. *Frit mallorquí* is a tasty mixture of strips of fried liver and kidney, peppers and leeks.

Meat

Every rural family on the island once kept pigs, and many still do. Pork and its by-products are a mainstay, therefore, including *botifarra* (a spicy sausage, either white or dark), *sobrasada*, a bright red, pork-and-red-pepper-sausage with a consistency rather like pâté, and *jamón serrano* or

Fresh ingredients for *cuina mallorquina*

jamón iberico, a delicious cured ham, cut from a whole piece hanging from the ceiling.

Other popular dishes are *llomb amb col* (pork with cabbage and raisins); and *arròs brut* (rice with pork or chicken). *Lechona asada* (roast suckling pig) is really a Christmas dish but may sometimes be found on menus at other times.

You don't see a great many cows in Mallorca, so there's not a lot of beef in the restaurants, although some of the more expensive places serve delicious steaks. Chicken – *pollo* – is fairly common, though, and goat – *cabrito* – turns up on country menus, usually grilled, sometimes in a stew. Rabbit *(conejo)*, is popular, sometimes served in a *greixonera* (stew), or *à la plancha* – grilled, and accompanied by *allioli,* a garlic mayonnaise; *conejo con caracoles*, rabbit with snails, is a favourite dish.

Snails *(caracoles)* are something of an acquired taste, but one that the islanders acquired long ago. At times they can be a free source of protein: after it has rained you'll see people out carrying string bags full of sand. They're looking for snails, which they clean by leaving them for several days in the sand, before cooking them and then eating them with *allioli*. Purists insist that true *allioli*, which is sometimes also served with the bread and olives that arrive at the start of a meal, should be made simply with oil and garlic, without the addition of eggs.

Fish

Really fresh fish and seafood are becoming something of a luxury on Mallorca. The seas have been over-fished and local fishermen, in any case, could not keep up with demand in summer. If you ask, waiters will usually tell you honestly that much of the fish they serve is imported, frozen, from Spain's Atlantic ports. *Salmonete* (red mullet) is caught locally, so are sardines *(sardinas)* and some of the *langostas*, spiny lobsters that are found on many menus. Locally caught *cap roig* – scorpion fish – is the choice Mallorcan fish; the cheeks are considered a great delicacy. *Caldereta de langosta* (*llagosta* in Mallorquí), a delicious lobster casserole, is a Menorquin dish, and an expensive one, that appears on some Mallorcan menus. *Zarzuela de mariscos* can be excellent – a thick stew of shellfish, tomatoes, garlic, wine and almonds.

Farmed trout *(trucha)*, sole *(lenguado)* and hake *(merluza)*, which are imported into the islands frozen, also feature. Squid *(calamares)*, cuttlefish *(sepia)* and octopus *(pulpo)*

Bread and Oil

Mallorca, whose landscape is dotted with ancient, gnarled olive trees and once-functional windmills, is renowned for its bread and oil – so much so that Tomás Graves, the son of Robert, has written a whole book about it. The bread is dense and biscuit coloured, the oil thick and rich and green. So it is not surprising that *pa amb oli*, bread and oil (pronounced *pamboli*), is served everywhere. It is simply toasted bread rubbed with garlic, sprinkled with salt and lubricated with olive oil. As a refinement it is also rubbed with fresh tomatoes *(pa amb tomàquet)* and served with cheese, local ham, *sobrasada (see page 97)* or even tuna. Cafés called *pambolierias* will give you your chosen ingredients on a large platter, plus a bottle of oil, and leave you to make yourself a tasty, filling and economical snack.

cooked in a variety of ways, are also widely available. *Calamares en su tinta* is squid cooked in its own ink; *a la romana* means it is cut into rings and fried in batter – excellent when fresh and not over-battered. *Bacalao* is cod, salted and dried, and not to everyone's taste, but when well prepared it can be good, especially in *esqueixada*, a salad of tomatoes, onions, beans and shredded salt cod.

Island Sweets and Puddings

Home-made *crema catalana*, or its mass-produced cousin, known as *flan*, is as ubiquitous in the Balearics as the mainland, but there are also some wonderful sweet pastries and the almond and honey desserts that are a legacy of the Moorish occupation. Fig cake, a rich, dark brown confection with the consistency of Christmas pudding, is particularly popular in and around Sóller, a town also known for its *picos de marzapan* – little white pyramids of marzipan. Vegetarians should be aware that lard *(saim)* is an essential Mallorcan ingredient. It is a key element in the *ensaimada*, the light, airy pastry that's rolled up like a turban, dusted with sugar, and eaten for breakfast, sometimes dipped in coffee.

> There is also fruit, of course; sweet melons, delicious juicy oranges, peaches and nectarines, fresh figs and grapes, all the better because they are locally grown and have ripened in the field, not in transit.

Drinks

Wine is usually drunk with meals, much of it imported from the Spanish mainland; Riojas and varieties from the Catalan Penedès region feature prominently. But island wines are good, too, and some restaurants (especially the *cellers*) specialise in them. Most come from the region around Binissalem, which lies between Palma and Inca.

Spanish beer is also popular, especially with young people. Fresh orange juice *(zumo de naranja)* is refreshing and delicious; and those who like the flavour of almonds should try *horchata de chufa*, a milky drink made from ground almonds that is served ice cold in summer. A local aperitif is *palo*, made from carobs and herbs and produced in Bunyola. You'll see the trade mark 'Palo Tunel' all over the island.

**Binissalem produces
a good range of wines**

Eating Habits

Local people eat late; lunch is between 1.30 and 4pm, and any time before 9.30 or 10pm is regarded as a bit early for dinner. However, restaurateurs, aware that northern European visitors like to eat earlier, have adapted their timetables accordingly. Remember that a restaurant that may look empty and unloved at 8pm may be packed and popular by 10pm. As breakfast is insubstantial – coffee and toast or a croissant – lunch is often the main meal. Islanders generally have three-courses, but it's perfectly acceptable to share a first course, or to order *un sólo plato* – just a main course.

Many restaurants offer a *menú del día*, a daily set menu that is a real bargain; this is always available at lunchtime, and sometimes in the evening as well. For a fixed price (around €10–12), you get three courses – a starter, often soup or salad, a main dish and dessert, which is usually ice-cream, a piece of fruit or a *flan*, plus bread and a glass of wine, beer or bottled

Alfresco dining

water. In restaurants where local people or Spanish visitors are eating, you will notice that many of them order the *menú*, which is an indication that it is not just one specially designed for tourists.

Reservations are necessary only at expensive restaurants or places that are popular for Sunday lunch. Prices sometimes include service – look for *servicio incluido* on the bill – but if not, it is customary to leave a 10 percent tip.

Tapas

Tapas, the snacks that have become popular far beyond the borders of Spain, form a major part of eating out in Mallorca – at least in the bigger towns. They are still eaten as snacks, with drinks, which was their original role, but it is now common for a selection of these small dishes, or *raciones*, which are larger portions, to take the place of a main meal and this can be a relatively inexpensive way to eat. The advantage is that it allows you to be adventurous without making too many mistakes. The size of portions varies quite a lot, so be guided by a waiter as to how many dishes to order. As well as meatballs *(albóndigas)* and mushrooms *(champiñones)* you can try stuffed squid *(calamares rellenos), pimientos de padrón* – small, green peppers grilled whole and sprinkled with sea salt; spicy *chorizo* or *espinacas à la catalana* – spinach cooked with garlic, anchovies, raisins and pine nuts. All are served with fresh bread to mop up the sauces and complement the strong flavours.

Bars and Cafés

Bars and cafés are an important institution in Spanish life. In towns, some open at first light to cater for early-morning workers and most are open by 8.30am for breakfast. One of the great pleasures of the Mediterranean is sitting in a square in the morning with a *café con leche* (coffee with milk) or *café solo* (black coffee) and a croissant or *ensaimada* and watching a town come to life. In resorts, however, where many bars are open late at night and many tourists breakfast in their hotels, you may have more difficulty finding somewhere for an early coffee.

Wines and spirits are served at all hours. It is usually 10 percent cheaper to have a drink at the bar rather than at a table. Sitting on a stool at the bar can make you feel like one of the locals, too, although it is not as relaxing as taking your place at an outside table and watching the world go by.

Trying a variety of tapas can add up to a satisfying meal

To Help you Order (in Spanish)

Could we have a table?	**¿Nos puede dar una mesa, por favor?**
Do you have a set menu?	**¿Tiene un menú del día?**
I would like...	**Quisiera…**
The bill, please	**La cuenta, por favor**

Deciphering the Menu

agua	water	**poco hecho**	rare
vino	wine	**al punto**	medium
leche	milk	**buen hecho**	well done
cerveza	beer	**asado**	roast
pan	bread	**a la plancha**	grilled
entremeses	hors-d'oeuvre	**al ajillo**	in garlic
ensalada	salad	**picante**	spicy
tortilla	omelette	**salsa**	sauce
pescado	fish	**cocido**	stew
mariscos	shellfish	**jamón serrano**	cured ham
langosta	lobster	**chorizo**	spicy sausage
calamares	squid	**morcilla**	black pudding
mejillones	mussels	**bocadillo**	sandwich
anchoas	anchovies	**arroz**	rice
atún	tuna	**verduras**	vegetables
bacalao	dried cod	**champiñones**	mushrooms
cangrejo	crab	**judías**	beans
pulpitos	baby octopus	**espinacas**	spinach
trucha	trout	**cebollas**	onions
carne	meat	**lentejas**	lentils
cerdo/lomo	pork	**queso**	cheese
ternera	veal	**postre**	dessert
cordero	lamb	**helado**	ice cream
buey/res	beef	**azúcar**	sugar
pollo	chicken	**flan**	caramel
conejo	rabbit		custard

HANDY TRAVEL TIPS

An A–Z Summary of Practical Information

A

ACCOMMODATION (See also CAMPING, and the list of RECOMMENDED HOTELS on pages 128–136)

Hotel prices are not government-controlled, but rates are posted at reception desks and in rooms. Off-season, you can often get lower rates, although many hotels in resort areas close between November and March. In season, the majority of resort hotels are block-booked by package tour operators.

Accommodation ranges across a broad spectrum, although there are few *pensions* (guest houses). *Hostales* (modest hotels) are graded from one to three stars while *hoteles* (hotels) are rated from one to five stars. Grades are more a reflection of facilities than quality: some two-star places can be superior to others with four.

A London-based company, Travel Intelligence, offers a personalised booking service, catering to clients' specific preferences (tel: 020 7580 2663, <www.travelintelligence.net>).

Small hotels in rural settings and refurbished farmhouses and manor houses are called *finca* or *agroturisme* properties. They range from rustic to luxurious; many have pools, tennis courts, and minimum 4- or 7-day stays; contact Agroturisme Balear, Avinguda Gabriel Alomar i Villalonga 8a, 2º, Palma, tel: 971 721 508, fax: 971 727 317, e-mail: agroturismo@mallorcanet.com for details. All-in package deals are the cheapest option and, while accommodation is usually in the busiest resorts, it can provide an economical base for exploring the island. Packages offering accommodation in apartments or villas are also popular. These are usually part of a complex with a pool, gardens and sports facilities. Finally, there is the option of staying in a monastery or sanctuary. There are about 15 of these (the *Where to Go* section gives details of several) and the tourist office in Palma *(see page 126)* can provide a full list. These are generally fairly austere but extremely economical and are popular with local people and outdoor enthusiasts.

Breakfast is often but not always included in a hotel room rate; check before booking. A value-added tax (IVA) of 7 percent is added to the total. A controversial eco-tax, introduced in 2002, which added approximately €1 per person per night to hotel accommodation, has since been suspended.

I would like a single/ double room	**Quisiera una habitación sencilla/doble**
With/without bathroom and toilet/shower	**con/sin baño/ducha**
What's the rate per night?	**¿Cuál es el precio por noche?**
Is breakfast included?	**¿Está incluído el desayuno?**

AIRPORT *(Aeropuerto)*

Palma de Mallorca's massive Son Sant Joan Airport (PMI) is about 11km (7 miles) from the city centre (tel: 971 789 000; <www.aena.es>). There is a tourist information desk in the Arrivals Hall (tel: 971 789 556). Taxis and regular buses link the airport with Palma. Bus No. 17 leaves the airport every 20 minutes from 6.10am to 1.30am, running to the centre of Palma, with stops en route, in approximately 30 minutes. Bus No. 1 goes to the port/ferry terminal. There is a bus stop outside the car park, in front of the Arrivals Hall. Tour-company representatives and coaches meet package-holiday passengers. There's a taxi rank outside the Arrivals Hall, and taxi drivers do the journey into Palma a lot faster than the bus, taking around 15–20 minutes. The approximate fare is €15.

B

BICYCLE AND SCOOTER HIRE *(Bicicletas de aquiler)*

A practical and enjoyable way to see the island is to hire a bicycle, and this can be done in most of the resorts – hotels and tourist offices have leaflets, and you'll be handed flyers in the street. Mopeds and scooters are also available, but you'll need a special licence. Prices vary widely, so shop around. Remember that a helmet is compulsory when riding a motorcycle, whatever the engine size. Ask the bike shop for a helmet and for a pump and puncture kit, in case you get stuck with a flat tyre many miles from your hotel.

BUDGETING FOR YOUR TRIP

Mallorca is relatively inexpensive compared to some European destinations, but in some respects more expensive than mainland Spain. All prices below are approximate and given only as a guide.

Accommodation. Hotels can be more expensive than on the Spanish mainland *(see approximate prices in Recommended Hotels, page 128)*. Rates for two sharing a double room during high season can range from as low as €35–40 in a *hostal* to as much as €400 at a top-of-the-range hotel. A comfortable, pleasant 3-star hotel will cost about €100. Rates drop considerably out of season.

Attractions. Most museums and galleries charge an entry fee of around €2.50–4.50; in Palma a combined ticket allows you to visit five museums for €10. Entry to La Real Cartuja, Valldemossa costs €7.50; the Coves del Drach and Coves d'Artà around €8. Water parks are more expensive, around €16–20, but these are places where families will spend a whole day. A 2-hour trip in a glass-bottomed boat costs around €14 (children half-price).

Car hire: With comprehensive insurance and tax, rates are around €35 a day with the big international companies; you get a better deal if you book for a week. Many competing firms in the resorts will offer lower rates; cars booked in advance via the Internet are also cheaper, around €180 for a week in high season *(see Car Hire)*.

Getting there: Air fares vary enormously. Flights from the UK with a budget airline can vary from around £95 return off-season to £180 or more in high season. Scheduled flights can be as low as £120 if you book well in advance, but anything up to £300 if you make a relatively late booking. The cheapest flights are usually available via the Internet, booked well in advance, or by taking a chance on a last-minute offer. From the US, flights cost approximately $660–$865.

Ferries: Inter-island ferries between Mallorca and Menorca are reasonable for foot passengers (about €65 return), but quite expensive if you take a car, about €225 for a car and two passengers.

Meals: The Spanish institution, the *menú del día*, a fixed price midday (and sometimes evening) meal, is usually an excellent bargain, costing around €10–12 for a reasonably good three-course meal with one drink included. In a bar a continental breakfast (fresh orange juice, coffee and croissant) will cost around €5. The average price of a three-course à la carte meal, including house wine, will be about €25–30 per person. You can pay considerably less, but at the top restaurants you may pay more than twice that much.

I want to change some pounds/dollars.	**Quiero cambiar libras/dólares.**
Do you accept travellers' cheques?	**¿Acepta usted cheques de viajero?**
Can I pay with this credit card?	**¿Puedo pagar con esta tarjeta de crédito?**

C

CAMPING (*Camping*)

Pitching a tent on beaches and parkland is illegal and you will be asked to move on. You may be able to camp on private land, but be sure to ask permission from the owner first.

There are two official camp sites, both in the north of the island: Club San Pedro, Artá (Colonia Sant Pere), tel: 971 589 023, fax: 971 730 448, open mid-May to mid-September, is 1.5km (1 mile) from the beach, with a swimming pool, hot and cold showers, bar/restaurant, and supermarket. Sun Club Picafort, Platja de Muro (Carretera Port de Alcúdia–Can Picafort), tel: 971 860 002, fax: 971 717 896, is open all year. The site is within walking distance of the beach and facilities include swimming pools, tennis courts, showers and baths, bars/restaurant, supermarket and disco. Both sites have a capacity for 500 pitches, but Sun Club Picafort is by far the better of the two in terms of site, facilities and maintenance. You are advised to book in advance for July and August. Camping is also permitted at the Santuario de Lluc, tel: 971 871 525.

CAR HIRE (Coches de alquiler)

The bus service is good, but if you want to travel a good deal around the island, hiring a car is advisable. Major international companies – Avis, Hertz, Budget, Europcar – and Spanish national hire companies have offices in the airport Arrivals Hall and in Palma as well as in the major resorts. Many agencies have weekly specials (all with unlimited mileage). These deals are very reasonable, sometimes as low as €25–28 per day. Rates are seasonal, and usually lower if organised in advance, especially over the Internet; <www.carjet.com> is a reliable online outfit. Find out what insurance is included – third-party is by law, but some charge more for comprehensive insurance – called *todo riesgo*. Be aware that insurance may not cover you for off-road driving, even in a four-wheel-drive vehicle. A value-added tax (IVA) of 15 percent is added to the total, but will have been included if you have booked in advance.

Most types and sizes of car are available, including four-wheel-drive vehicles, but the vast majority are small economy models, well suited to small parking spaces, narrow rural roads and mountain bends. Most have air conditioning but check when you book.

Hirers must be at least 21 and have held a licence for six months. Hire companies will accept your national driver's licence, so you don't need an international one. Some companies impose a surcharge of up to €10 for renting at the airport or for delivering a car to your hotel; others include it in the quoted price.

I'd like to rent a car.	**Quisiera alquilar un coche.**
for one day/week.	**por un día/una semana.**
Please include full insurance.	**Haga el favor de incluir el seguro a todo riesgo.**

CLIMATE (*Clima*)

The sea is pleasantly warm for swimming from June to October. July and August can be scorching and humidity may be high. Mallorca enjoys a mild winter, too, and more and more hotels are staying open during the winter months. It can be chilly and wet at times but a wall of mountains along the northwest coast protects the rest of the island from the worst of the winter weather. The tourist season is getting longer: spring and autumn bring walkers and bird watchers, and those who enjoy sightseeing in milder temperatures.

The average temperatures below apply to Palma, but do not vary greatly throughout the islands, except in the mountainous areas.

	J	F	M	A	M	J	J	A	S	O	N	D
°C	10	11	12	14	17	22	24	24	22	18	14	12
°F	50	51	54	58	63	71	76	76	72	65	57	53

CLOTHING (*Ropa*)

In summer the days are invariably very warm and you only need lightweight cotton clothes – although in June and September you may need a jacket or sweater for the evening. Remember also to take a sunhat and something with sleeves to cover your shoulders against the strong midday sun. During the rest of the year a light jacket and an umbrella will come in handy.

Although the tendency is towards casual dress, some restaurants, bars and clubs object to men wearing shorts and T-shirts and women being too skimpily dressed. Don't offend local sensibilities by wearing unsuitable clothes in city streets, museums or churches.

Walking shoes or good-quality trainers are advisable, of course, if you are planning any long treks; and take a small backpack to carry lightweight anoraks and refreshments.

CRIME AND SAFETY (See also EMERGENCIES)

Spain's crime rate has caught up with that of other European countries and the Balearics have not been immune, although they remain one of the safest places in Europe. Be on your guard against purse-snatchers and pickpockets near Palma Cathedral and around the Plaça Major at night, and in markets and other crowded places.

The rules are the ones you should follow almost anywhere. Don't leave valuables unattended, don't take them to the beach or leave them visible in a car. Make use of hotel safe-boxes where possible. Don't carry large sums of money or wear expensive jewellery, and keep hold of your camera. Be especially careful when getting money from automatic cash machines.

In Palma, report thefts and break-ins to the Policía Nacional, elsewhere to the Guardia Civil.

I want to report a theft.	**Quiero denunciar un robo.**

CUSTOMS AND ENTRY REQUIREMENTS (*Aduana*; see also EMBASSIES AND CONSULATES)

Citizens of the UK, US, Canada, Australia and New Zealand need only a valid passport to enter Spain and the Balearics for a stay of up to 90 days. Citizens of South Africa need a visa. Full information on passport and visa regulations is available from the Spanish Embassy in your own country.

As Spain is part of the European Union (EU), free exchange of non-duty-free items for personal use is permitted between Spain and other EU countries. However, duty-free items are still subject to restrictions. There are no limits on the amount of currency, Spanish or foreign, that you may import, although you should declare sums over the equivalent of €30,000.

D

DRIVING (*En coche*)

Road Conditions. Main roads are well surfaced, and there is a stretch of motorway around the city and the bay and up to Inca, and a stretch of tunnel through the mountains (toll charged) from Sóller towards Palma. There's a good straight road running east–west across the island and from Inca to Alcúdia. Secondary roads are narrow but generally good; on the mountainous northwest coast they have more hairpin bends than some drivers would like which demand concentration.

Rules and Regulations. The rules are the same as throughout Spain: Drive on the right, overtake on the left, yield to vehicles coming from the right (unless your road is marked as having priority). Seat belts are compulsory. Children under 10 must travel in the rear. Always carry your driving licence with you. It is a good idea to have a photocopy of your passport.

Speed limits. 120 km/h (75 mph) on motorways, 100 km/h (60 mph) on two-lane highways, 90 km/h (56mph) on other main roads, 50 km/h (32 mph), or as marked, in densely populated areas.

Traffic police. Roads are patrolled by the Traffic Civil Guard (Guardia Civil de Tráfico) on motorcycles. They are generally courteous and helpful, but they are also tough on lawbreakers. Fines are payable on the spot. Don't drink and drive. Apart from safety considerations, the permitted blood-alcohol level is low and penalties are stiff.

Fuel. Service stations are plentiful. Petrol (*gasolina*) comes in 90 (super lead-free) and 98 (lead-free super plus) grades. Diesel fuel is widely available. Fuel is slightly cheaper than in the UK but will seem expensive to US visitors.

Parking. Finding a place to park is difficult in Palma, but less so elsewhere. Most towns have 'blue zone' metered areas, denoted by a 'P' and blue lines on the road. There are also public car parks.

Mechanical problems. Garages are efficient, but repairs may take time in busy areas. For emergencies, call the Real Club Automóvil (tel: 971 750 110 or tel: 062).

Road signs. Most signs are the standard European pictographs, but you may encounter the following in Spanish or amended into Catalan/Mallorquí; the subsequent phrases in the list may also be useful.

Aparcamiento	Parking
Desviación	Detour
Obras	Road works
Peatones	Pedestrians
Peligro	Danger
Salida de camiones	Truck exit
Senso único	One way
Useful expressions:	
¿Se puede aparcar aqui?	Can I park here?
Llénelo, por favor.	Fill the tank please.
Ha habido un accidente.	There has been an accident.

E

ELECTRICITY (*Corriente eléctrica*)

The 220-v system is now standard. Sockets (outlets) take round, two-pin plugs, so you will probably need an international adapter plug, easily found in UK chemists and supermarkets and at airports. North American visitors will need a transformer unless they have dual-voltage appliances.

EMBASSIES AND CONSULATES *(Embajadas y consulados)*

Canada: For minor matters contact the British consulate in Palma *(see below)*. Other cases: Consulate General, Edificio Goya, Calle Núñez de Balboa 35, Madrid, tel: 914 233 250; fax: 914 233 251.
Ireland: (Honorary Consul) Carrer Sant Miquel 68, 8ª, Palma, tel: 971 719 244.
UK: Plaça Major 3-D, Palma, tel: 971 712 445/971 716 048, fax: 971 717 520.
US: Edificio Reina Constanza, Passeig Marítim (Porto Pi), 8, 9-D, Palma, tel: 971 403 707, fax: 971 403 971.

Where is the British/American consulate?	**¿Dónde está el consulado británico/americano?**

EMERGENCIES (See also EMBASSIES, HEALTH AND POLICE)

General emergency number (police, fire, ambulance): 112
National Police: 091
Municipal Police: 092
Guardia Civil (traffic): 062
Ambulance: 061
Fire: 080

Police!	**Policía!**
Help!	**Socorro!**
Fire!	**Fuego!**
Stop!	**Deténgase!**
Go away!	**Váyase!**

G

GAY AND LESBIAN TRAVELLERS (*Viajeros gay*)

The Balearics are among the most hospitable places in Spain for gay travellers. Mallorca has a number of establishments, including hotels, bars, discos and restaurants, that cater for gays or are gay-friendly. For detailed information, contact Ben Amics, the Gay and Lesbian Association of the Balearics, Apartado de Correos 469, Carrer Conquistador 2, Palma, tel: 971 723 058, toll-free 900 777 500, Mon–Fri 7–9pm, e-mail benamics@benamics.com, <www. benamics.com>. At the tourist office in Palma you can pick up a map showing the location of gay-friendly beaches, clubs, bars, etc.

GETTING TO MALLORCA

Air Travel *(see also Airports)*. Palma de Mallorca's airport is linked by regular scheduled non-stop flights from London, Dublin Berlin and Frankfurt, with frequent flights from many other European cities; from Belfast you need to go via Gatwick/Heathrow and/or Barcelona or Madrid. Flights from the US and Canada also go via London airports and Barcelona or Madrid; flight time from New York is approximately 10–12 hours. In the US contact Iberia, tel: 1-800 772 4642, <www.iberia.com/ibusa>; Continental Airlines, tel: 1-800 231 0856, <www.flycontinental.com>. In Canada, contact British Airways, tel: 1-800 668 1059, <www.ba.com>; Iberia, tel: 1-800 423 7421 (website as above). From Australia and New Zealand, flights usually go via London, where you can get a connecting flight to Palma.

For scheduled flights from the UK, contact Iberia, the Spanish national carrier, tel: 0845 850 9000, <www.iberia.com>; British Airways, tel: 0845 773 3377, <www.ba.com>; Spanair (now part of Star Alliance group), tel: 0870 6070 555, <www.spanair.es>. From Eire, contact Aer Lingus, tel: 0818 365 000, <www. aerlingus.com>.

Numerous budget airlines fly to Palma from airports all over the UK. Excellent bargains may be available if you travel at very short notice, both for flight-only tickets and for packages that include accommodation. Booking via the Internet is usually the cheapest method for flight-only tickets.

By Sea. Car ferries operate daily from Barcelona and Valencia to Palma. The slower, overnight trip takes 8 hours on Trasmediterránea (Moll de Paraires, Estació Marítim 2, tel: 902 454 645 or 971 702 300/971 366 050 in Palma; <www.trasmediterranea.com>); during peak holiday season it also operates a faster ferry, which takes 4½ hours. Baleària has a fast ferry from Barcelona to Alcúdia on Saturday and Sunday, which takes 3½ hours (tel: 902 160 180, <www.balearia.net>) and a slower one via Menorca on weekdays (5½ hours). Faster yet is the Buquebus (Moll de Paraires, Estació Marítim 3, tel: 934 817 360 in Barcelona or 971 400 969 in Palma; e-mail <reserves@buquebus.es>), which takes 3 hours.

H

HEALTH AND MEDICAL CARE (*Salud; atención médica*)

Standards of hygiene are generally high; the most common problems visitors encounter will be due to an excess of sun or alcohol. Bottled water is always safest, and is available, cheaply, almost everywhere. *Agua con gas* is carbonated, *agua sin gas* is still.

There are doctors in all towns and consulting hours are usually displayed. For less serious matters, first-aid personnel (*practicantes*) make daily rounds of the larger resort hotels; some hotels have a nurse on duty. Many resorts have medical centres (*centros medicos*), privately-run institutions which must be paid on the spot, in cash or by credit card (roughly €50/£32 a consultation).

It is always advisable to take out insurance to cover the risk of illness or accident when on holiday. UK residents can get a E111 form (available from post offices) which entitles residents of EU member states to reciprocal health arrangements, but it is only accepted by certain doctors/hospitals and in certain cases.

Pharmacies (*farmácias*) are open during normal shopping hours, but there is at least one – the *farmácia de guardia* – open all night in Palma and in the large resorts. In small towns, it may be difficult to find an after-hours pharmacy. A list of the pharmacy on rota duty is posted in chemists' windows. Spanish pharmacists are highly trained and generally speak some English; they can dispense drugs over the counter that would often need a prescription elsewhere.

In Palma, the Farmácia March on Carrer Joan Miró (opposite McDonald's) is open 24 hours a day, 365 days a year.

Emergency medical assistance can be obtained by dialling **112** or **061** (Ambulance), or tel: 295 000 – Creu Roja (Red Cross) ambulance service.

Major hospitals in Palma include:

Centro Médico, Edificio Reina Constanza, Passeig Marítim (Porto Pi) 8, tel: 971 707 035/55, fax: 971 707 056 (many of the staff speak English).

Hospital de la Creu Roja Espanyola, Carrer Pons i Gallarça 90, tel: 971 751 445.

Where's the nearest (all-night) chemist?	**¿Dónde está la farmácia (de guardia) más cercana?**
I need a doctor/ dentist.	**Necesito un médico/ dentista.**
sunburn/ sunstroke	**quemadura del sol/ una insolación**
an upset stomach	**molestias de estómago**

HOLIDAYS *(Fiestas)*

The following are official public holidays. There are a number of other holidays, usually saints' days, dotted throughout the year.

1 January	Año Nuevo	New Year's Day
6 January	Epifanía	Epiphany
20 January	San Sebastián	St Sebastian's Day
1 May	Día del Trabajo	Labour Day
25 July	Santiago Apóstol	St James's Day
15 August	Asunción	Assumption
12 October	Día de la Hispanidad	National Day
1 November	Todos los Santos	All Saints' Day
6 December	Día de la Española	Constitution Day
8 December	Inmaculada Concepción	Immaculate Conception
25 December	Navidad	Christmas Day

Movable dates:

Late March/April	Jueves Santo	Maundy Thursday
Late March/April	Viernes Santo	Good Friday
Late March/April	Lunes de Pascua	Easter Monday
Mid-June	Corpus Christi	Corpus Christi

L

LANGUAGE (*Idioma; lenguaje*)

While Castilian Spanish is the national language of Spain, a local form of Catalan – Mallorquí – is more widely spoken, and almost all islanders speak both. Most street signs appear only in Catalan. If you know some Spanish, you'll be fine; although the effort to speak Catalan is appreciated, it is not necessary. English and German are widely understood in resort areas.

The *Berlitz Spanish-English/English-Spanish Pocket Dictionary* covers most of the situations you may encounter during your travels.

Do you speak English?	**¿Habla usted inglés?**
I don't speak Spanish.	**No hablo español.**

M

MAPS (*Mapa* = country/regional map; *plano* = town map)

The maps of the island and cities produced by the tourism board and available at all tourist information offices should be sufficient, even for those travelling by car. Even though some roads are not labelled by number or name on the map, they are easy to identify and all roads are clearly indicated. A good place for more specific maps is La Casa de la Mapa, Carrer Sant Domingo 13, Palma.

Do you have a map of the city/island?	**¿Tiene un plano de la ciudad/isla?**

MEDIA (*Periódico* = newspaper; *revista* = magazine)

In the main tourist areas most English and German newspapers are sold on the day of publication. The Paris-based *International Herald Tribune* and the European edition of the *Wall Street Journal* are available on the day of publication. *USA Today* is widely available, as are the principal European and American magazines.

The *Majorca Daily Bulletin* is an English-language publication that concentrates mainly on local news but does cover UK and some international news as well. It has a useful What's On section, too. For Spanish speakers, the *Diario de Mallorca* and all the Spanish national newspapers and magazines are available.

Most hotels and bars have television, usually tuned to sports (international or local), and broadcasting in Castilian, Catalan (from Barcelona) and Mallorquí. Satellite dishes are sprouting and most tourist hotels offer multiple channels (German, French, Sky, BBC, CNN, etc.). Reception of the BBC World Service radio is usually good. A good set will (at times, at least) receive the BBC long-wave and even medium-wave domestic programmes. The Palma local radio station broadcasts in English 24 hours a day on 103.2 FM.

MONEY (*Dinero*)

Currency. Since 2002, Spain's monetary unit has been the euro (€), which is divided into 100 cents. Bank notes are available in denominations of 5, 10, 20, 50, 100, 200 and 500 euros, and there are coins for 1 and 2 euros and for 1, 2, 5, 10, 20 and 50 cents.

Currency exchange. Banks are the best place to exchange currency as they offer the best rates and charge no commission. A large number of travel agencies exchange foreign currency, and *casas de cambio* stay open outside banking hours. Be wary, however, of those advertising 'no commission' – their rates are much lower than those offered elsewhere, so you are in effect paying a hefty commission. Both banks and exchange offices pay slightly less for cash than for travellers' cheques. Always take your passport as proof of identity when you go to change money.

Credit cards. Major international cards are widely recognised, but smaller businesses tend to prefer cash. Visa/Eurocard/MasterCard are the most generally accepted. Credit and debit cards are also useful for obtaining cash from ATMs – cash machines – which are found in all towns and resorts. They offer the most convenient way of obtaining cash and will usually give you the best exchange rate.

Travellers' cheques. The majority of hotels, shops, restaurants, and travel agencies cash travellers' cheques, and so do banks, where

Where's the nearest bank/ currency exchange office?	**¿Dónde está el banco más cercano/la oficina de cambio más cercana?**
I want to change some dollars/pounds.	**Quiero cambiar dólares/ libres esterlina.**
Do you accept travellers' cheques?	**¿Acepta usted cheques de viajero?**
Can I pay with this credit card?	**¿Puedo pagar con esta tarjeta de crédito?**

you're likely to get a better rate (you will need your passport). It is safest to cash small amounts at a time, thereby keeping some of your funds in cheques, in the hotel safe. Keep a note of your unused cheque numbers somewhere safe and separate from the cheques, just in case of theft or other loss.

O

OPENING HOURS (*Horario*)

Most shops and offices are open from 9am to 1pm and again from 4 or 5pm until 8pm. Many museums and other tourist attractions maintain the same schedule, although increasingly the more popular ones are staying open throughout the day. The hours of the major museums are given in the relevant section of this guide. Large supermarkets and department stores usually stay open throughout the day and some until 10pm.

Post offices are usually open Monday to Friday 9am–2pm, but the main post office in Palma *(see next page)* opens in the afternoon as well, and on Saturday 9am–1pm. Banks generally open Monday to Friday 9am–2pm, and on Saturday 9am–1pm in winter only.

Restaurants serve lunch from 1–3.30pm. In the evenings timing depends on the kind of customers they expect. Local people usually eat between 9.30 and 11pm. Places catering for foreigners may function from 7pm, and many serve food throughout the afternoon.

P

POLICE (*Policía*)

Spanish municipal and national police are efficient, strict and courteous – and generally very responsive to issues involving foreign tourists. Dial 092 for municipal police and 091 for national police. The general emergency number is 112. The municipal police station in Palma is located at Carrer Ruíz de Alda 8.

POST OFFICES (*Correos*)

Identified by yellow and white signs with a crown and the words Correos y Telégrafos, post offices are for mail and telegrams; you can't telephone from them (<www.correos.es> for information). The postal system is pretty reliable and efficient. Special delivery is always a good idea if you want to make really sure of a speedy delivery. Opening hours are usually Monday to Friday 9am–2pm. The main post office in Palma is in Carrer Constitució 5 (off Passeig des Born), tel: 971 721 867, and stays open in the afternoon and on Saturday 9am–1pm. Stamps (*sellos*) are also sold by tobacconists (*estanco/tabacos*) and by most shops selling postcards.

Where is the (nearest) post office?	**¿Dónde está la oficina de correos (más cercana)?**
A stamp for this letter/ postcard, please.	**Por favor, un sello para esta carta/tarjeta.**

PUBLIC TRANSPORT (*Transporte público*)

Mallorca has a reliable and comprehensive transport system serving almost all towns and villages. You can get a bus and train timetable from the tourist information offices in Palma and Sóller (*see page 126*), or tel: 971 176 970. A combined bus and train ticket is available. Most public services end fairly early, around 8.45pm.

Bus (*autobús*). Mallorca is well served by bus lines; its vehicles are clean and easy to use and drivers are generally helpful. Destinations are marked on the front of the bus and each town has its own bus station or terminal. In Palma, most services begin their journeys at the Plaça d'Espanya or the new bus station close by in Carrer Eusebio Estada (near the railway station). City buses are also efficient. There is a set fare for city journeys and you buy your ticket on the bus. A Palma bus schedule (from Empresa Municipal de Transports, EMT) detailing city routes is available from the tourist office.

Train *(tren)*. Mallorca has two narrow-gauge lines, which start from adjoining stations on Plaça d'Espanya in Palma. The first line goes to Inca, and some trains now continue to Sa Pobla and Manacor, while the more picturesque one links Palma and Sóller. It makes six runs in each direction every day (seven on Sunday). The *tren turístic* (10.40am and 12.15pm) makes an extra stop at an overlook for a photo-opportunity, but charges twice the normal fare. For Inca trains, tel: 971 752 245; for Sóller trains, tel: 971 752 051.

Ferries. Passenger ferries to Menorca go between Cala Ratjada and Ciutadella (Cape Balear Cruceros, tel: 971 818 517). The journey takes about 75 minutes and there are some good deals, including some that offer inclusive bus journeys to and from Palma. Car ferries run twice a day (except Saturday) between Port d'Alcúdia and Ciutadella and take around 2¾ hours (Iscomar Ferries; tel: 902 119 128; fax: 971 707 721, <www.iscomar.com>). Baleària has daily connections between Alcúdia and Ciutadella and Maó, tel: 902 160 180, <www.balearia.net>.

Taxi. Taxi prices compare favourably with those in many other places. Taxis are a good way to get around Palma if you are visiting places outside the centre. Check the fare before you get in; rates are fixed and displayed in several languages on the window.

> How much is it to the centre of town?   ¿Cuanto es al centro?

R

RELIGION *(Religión)*

Catholicism is the religion of Spain and there are churches all over the island. When visiting churches as a tourist, dress modestly and respect the privacy of those who are there to pray. In Palma there are churches representing most major faiths; the tourist offices have information on religious services, including those in foreign languages.

T

TELEPHONES *(Teléfonos)*

Spain's country code is 34. The local area code is 971 and must be dialled before all phone numbers, even for local calls.

The telephone office is independent of the post office and is identified by a blue and white sign. You can make direct-dial local and international calls from public telephone booths *(cabinas)* in the street. Most operate with both coins and cards; international telephone credit cards can also be used. Instructions for use are given in several languages in the booths. You can also make calls at public telephone offices called *locutorios*. This is much quieter than making a call on the street, and more convenient, as an attendant will place the call for you, and you pay afterwards.

For calls at pay phones, it's wise to use a phone card *(tarjeta telefónica)*, which can be purchased at any *estanco* (tobacconist's shop). To make an international call, dial 00 for an international line plus the country code plus the phone number, omitting any initial zero. Calls are cheaper after 10pm on weekdays, after 2pm on Saturday, and all day Sunday. Fax machines can be found in communication centres in most holiday resorts.

TIME DIFFERENCES *(Huso horario)*

The Balearics keep the same time as mainland Spain, which is one hour ahead of GMT, so Spanish time is generally one hour ahead of London, the same as Paris and six hours ahead of New York.

TIPPING *(Propinas)*

A service charge is sometimes included on restaurant bills *(servicio incluido)*. If not, it is usual to tip waiters 10 percent, and taxi drivers a similar amount; it's normal to leave a few coins, rounding up the bill, at a bar counter. Porters, hairdressers and chambermaids should be given €1–2.

TOILETS (*Servicios*)

There are many expressions for toilets in Spanish: *aseos, servicios, lavabos, wc* and *bater*. The first three are the most common. Toilet doors usually have a 'C' for *Caballeros* (gentlemen), an 'S' for *Señoras* (ladies). Public toilets exist in some large towns but they are rare; most bars will allow you to use their facilities. Those that object usually keep the key behind the bar.

TOURIST INFORMATION OFFICES
(*Oficinas de información turística*)

Tourist Offices Abroad
Canada: 2 Bloor Street West, Suite 3402, Toronto, Ontario M4W 3E2, tel: 1416-961 3131, <www.tourspaintoronto.on.ca>.
UK: 22–23 Manchester Square, London W1U 3PX, tel: 020 7486 8077; brochure line, tel: 09063 640 630, email: info.londres@tourspain.es; <www.tourspain.co.uk>.
US:Water Tower Place, Suite 915 East, 845 North Michigan Avenue, Chicago, IL 60611, tel: 312-944 0216/642 1992.
8383 Wilshire Boulevard, Suite 960, Beverly Hills, CA 90211, tel: 213-658 7188, fax: 213-658 1061.
666 5th Avenue, 35th floor, New York, NY 10103, tel: 212-265 8822, fax: 212 265 8864, <www.okspain.org>.
1221 Brickell Avenue, Miami, FL 33131, tel: 305-358 1992.

Tourist Offices in Mallorca
Palma: Aeroport Son Sant Joan, tel: 971 789 556; Plaça de la Reina 2, tel: 971 712 216; Plaça d'Espanya, tel: 971 754 329; Carrer Constitució 1, tel: 971 725 396.
Municipal Tourist Office (for information on Palma only): Carrer Sant Domingo 11, Palma, tel: 971 724 090.
Cala Ratjada: Plaça dels Pins, tel: 971 563 033.
Sóller: Plaça Sa Constitució 1, tel: 971 630 200.
Pollença: Carrer Sant Domingo 2, tel: 971 535 077.

TRAVELLERS WITH DISABILITIES (*Los discapacitados*)

Palma airport and most modern hotels have wheelchair access and facilities for travellers with disabilities. For more general information, consult the online magazine *Disability View*, Craven Publishing 15–39 Durham Street, Kinning Park, Glasgow GW1 1BS, tel: 0141 419 0044, fax: 0141 419 0077, <www.disabilityview.co.uk>, e-mail: info@disabilityview.co.uk.

W

WEBSITES AND INTERNET CAFÉS

There are several Balearic sites you could log on to, including:
<www.mallorca.com> general information
<www.spainalive.com/mallorca> general information
<www.fehm.es> Hotel Federation of Mallorca
<www.mallorcaonline.com> hotel and general information
<www.agroturismo-mallorca.com> rural tourism properties
<www.aena.es> Palma airport information

There are Internet cafés all over the island. A couple of good ones in Palma are: Hostal Ritzi, Carrer Apuntadors 6, tel: 971 714 610, e-mail: bigbyte@HostalRitzi; L@Red Cybercafé, Carrer Concepció 5, e-mail: nat@laredcafe.com. In the resorts Internet cafés tend to come and go, but there are always easy-to-find places in the commercial centres.

Y

YOUTH HOSTELS (*Albergues juveniles*)

There are two youth hostels but they are sometimes booked by groups in summer, so reserve in advance. Alberg Juvenil La Victoria, Carretera Cabo Pinar s/n, Alcúdia, tel/fax: 971 545 395; closed Nov–Mar. Alberg Platja de Palma, Carrer Costa Brava 17, Platja de Palma, tel/fax: 971 260 892; open all year.

Recommended Hotels

There is a wide range of accommodation available, from luxury hotels to small, family-run hostels, as well as the huge, impersonal, but usually very efficient modern hotels in the bigger resorts, where much of the accommodation is block-booked by tour companies. Some hotels close for a few months in winter, so finding inexpensive off-season accommodation isn't always easy. This will be indicated in the listings below. For details on rural *(agroturismo)* holidays and staying in hermitages and sanctuaries, *see page 106*.

Some hotel rates include breakfast and IVA, the 7 percent value-added tax, but it is not standard, so it is wise to check. A short-lived €1 per head eco-tax on hotel guests has now been suspended. Website addresses are given only when they are specific to the hotel, rather than reservation agencies. The following guide indicates prices for a double room in high season (prices should be used as an approximate guide only):

€€€€	over 240 euros
€€€	120–240 euros
€€	60–120 euros
€	below 60 euros

PALMA

Almudaina €€ *Avinguda Jaume III 9, tel: 971 727 340, fax: 971 722 599.* Comfortable and moderately priced, with obliging staff, this central hotel is on Palma's foremost shopping street. Established in 1972, it was completely renovated 20 years later. Rooms on upper floors have magnificent views over the city.

Born €€ *Carrer Sant Jaume 3, tel: 971 712 942, fax: 971 718 618, <www.hotelborn.com>.* In a restored 16th-century palace just off Plaça Rei Joan Carles II, this is one of Palma's best bargains. With a grand central staircase and beautiful courtyard under Romanesque-style arches, it is full of atmosphere. Understandably popular, so advance reservations are essential.

Convent de la Missió €€€ *Carrer de la Missió 7, tel: 971 227 347, <www.conventdelamissio.com>.* New in 2003, this stylish hotel, in a converted 17th-century convent in the old quarter, has light, airy rooms, a roof terrace, a sauna and an excellent restaurant.

Dalt Murada €€ *Carrer Almudaina 6, tel: 971 425 300, fax: 971 719 708, <www.hoteldaltmurada.com>.* In a restored manor house close to the cathedral (the name means 'high walls'), this attractive little hotel has a friendly atmosphere and a garden and provides bathrobes for guests' use. Advance reservations recommended.

Palacio Ca Sa Galesa €€€€ *Miramar 8, tel: 971 715 400, fax: 971 721 579, <www.palaciocasagalesa.com>.* Housed in a grand, meticulously restored 17th-century palace, this tiny hotel is furnished with antiques, has terraces with views, a Roman-style indoor pool, jacuzzi and saunas. Wheelchair access.

San Lorenzo €€€–€€€€ *Carrer San Lorenzo 14, tel: 971 728 200, fax: 971 711 901, <www.hotelsanlorenzo.com>.* This enchanting little hotel (only 6 rooms) in a lively section of town is always booked well in advance. Excellent value, rooms individually decorated; all have balconies, some have garden access. Small pool.

Ritzi € *Carrer Apuntadors 6, tel/fax: 971 714 610.* Good, basic hostel in the restaurant quarter, popular with backpackers. Some of the 12 rooms have shared bathrooms. There is an Internet café on the ground floor.

THE WESTERN CORNER

Banyalbufar

Baronia € *Carrer Major s/n, tel/fax: 971 618 146.* This endearingly simple hotel, set among terraced hills, was originally part of a 17th-century baronial tower. The rooms are a little on the spartan side, but adequate, and they all have terraces. Pleasant pool. Closed November–April.

Mar i Vent €€ *Carrer Major 49, tel: 971 618 000, fax: 971 618 201, <www.hotelmarivent.com>*. Mar i Vent is an attractive family-owned hotel atop a cliff with restaurant, terrace, garden and swimming pool. It has comfortable rooms and stunning sea views. A path leads down to two quiet coves. Also does half board. Closed December–January.

Illetes

Bon Sol €€€€ *Paseo de Illetas 30, tel: 971 402 111, fax: 971 402 559*. A family-run, antique-filled hotel situated on multiple levels, cascading down pine-shaded cliffs to its own secluded beach. Other facilities include restaurant, sun terraces and swimming pool. Closed mid-November–mid-December.

Portals Nous

Bendinat €€€€ *Carrer Andres Ferret Sobral 1, tel: 971 675 725, fax: 971 677 276, <www.hotelbendinat.es>*. A mid-sized and handsome hacienda-style hotel in a small, rocky cove in this exclusive area. There are rooms with balconies and bungalows amid terraced gardens. Close to five golf courses. Closed November–February.

Port d'Andratx

Brismar €–€€ *Almirante Riera Alemany 6, tel: 971 671 600, fax: 971 671 183*. This comfortable and simple seafront hotel is a bargain given the coveted location. Ask for a room with a view of the harbour, although these are the noisiest. Has a good family-style restaurant and terrace. Wheelchair access.

THE WEST COAST

Deià

Es Molí €€€€ *Carretera Valldemossa–Deià s/n, Deià, tel: 971 639 000, fax: 971 639 333, <www.esmoli.com>*. An elegant hotel in a converted 19th-century manor house on a hill just outside Deià, with incomparable views of the village and the sea. The pool is spring-fed, and the hotel is set in 1.5 hectares (4 acres) of gardens. The service is splendid. Breakfast on the terrace. The highly recommended restaurant, Ca'n Quet, has its own garden. Closed November–mid-April.

Fonda Villa Verde €€ *Carrer Ramón Llull, Deià, tel: 971 639 037, fax: 971 639 485.* A simple, friendly little place with a family atmosphere, situated close to the church, with a delightful garden/terrace. Closed December–February. Cash only.

La Residencia €€€€ *Son Moragues, Deià, tel: 971 639 011, fax: 971 639 370, e-mail: reservas@laresidencia.com.* This elegant hotel, owned by Virgin boss Richard Branson, is superbly located in two 16th-century manor houses. A chic international clientele enjoys a health and beauty centre, beautiful pools, tennis courts, and El Olivo, one of the island's finest restaurants (*see page 140*).

Miramar €€ *Carrer Ca'n Oliver s/n, Deià, tel/fax: 971 639 084, <www.pensionmiramar.com>.* Set above the main road running through the village, up a narrow track, this pleasant little *hostal* has a cavernous entrance hall and rooms with and without bathrooms. Breakfast, which is included in the price, is served on the terrace. Cash only.

S'Hotel d'es Puig €€ *Es Puig 4, Deià, tel: 971 639 409, fax: 971 639 210, <www.hoteldespuig.com>.* Tucked away on the stone streets of Deià this delightful little hotel has airy rooms, a serve-yourself bar, a small pool and a relaxed and friendly atmosphere. It also has four apartments to let in a nearby house, and the tenants can use the hotel pool. Closed mid-November–February.

Llucalcari
Costa d'Or €€ *tel: 971 639 025, fax: 971 639 347, <www.hoposa. es/pagingles/hcostadori.htm>.* Down a track just outside Deià, this secluded hotel has pinewoods running down to the beach and a pool set high above the sea. Large restaurant, small outside bar. Completely renovated in 2004. Closed November–March.

Port de Sóller

Es Port €€ *Antonio Montis s/n, Port de Sóller, tel: 971 631 650, fax: 971 631 662.* A large, attractive hotel, one of the first to be established in the area, with gardens, sun terraces and a great view over the port. Comfortable rooms and splendid grounds. There's a huge olive press in the bar. Heated pools; thalassotherapy service. Close to the bus and tram routes. Wheelchair access.

Sóller

Ca n'Aí Hotel Rural €€€ *Camí de Son Sales 50 (Cta Sóller–Deià), Sóller, tel: 971 632 494, fax: 971 631 899, <www.canai. com>.* A restored manor house with beams and whitewashed walls, surrounded by orange groves and with little canals running through the grounds. Eleven suites with terraces. Pool and jacuzzi. Also offers half- and full-board. Closed November–January.

Ca'n Mario € *Carrer Uetam 8, Valldemossa, tel: 971 612 122, fax: 971 616 029.* A simple, old-fashioned *hostal*, with plants and colourful tiles on the central staircase. Conveniently situated in the centre of Valldemossa, it has a restaurant serving good local food. Reservations essential as there are only eight rooms.

El Guía €€ *Carrer Castanyer 2 Sóller, tel/fax: 971 630 227.* This pleasant, down-to-earth hotel offers excellent value. Attractive courtyard and a good restaurant. Near the railway station. Closed November–April.

Hostal Residencia Margarita Trías Vives € *Carrer Reial 3, Sóller, tel: 971 634 214.* A small guesthouse close to the station. The 10 rooms are pleasant but not en suite. A good budget option in this attractive little town. Closed November–March.

THE NORTH

Alcúdia

Parc Natural €€€ *Platja de Muro, Carretera Alcúdia–Artà, tel: 971 892 017, fax: 971 890 345.* Externally, this large modern hotel is not appealing, but the rooms are well furnished and comfortable and it has all the facilities you would expect. Although it's on the main road, it has the sweep of sandy beach on one side and the Parc S'Albufera on the other.

Cala Sant Vicenç

Cala Sant Vicenç €€€ *Carrer Maressers 2, tel: 971 530 250, central reservations: tel: 958 227 019, fax: 971 532 084, <www.hotel-cala.com>*. A beautifully renovated, family-owned Relais & Chateaux property in this stunning little bay. Relaxed but extremely efficient. Gym and fitness centre; landscaped pool. The Cavall Bernat restaurant is recommended. No children under 14. Closed December–January. Wheelchair access.

Niu €€€ *Cala Barques s/n, tel: 971 530 100, fax: 971 531 220*. A pleasant, owner-managed, modern hotel overlooking the lovely cove of Cala Sant Vicenç. The simple facilities include terraces, bar and an excellent restaurant specialising in fish and lobster. Reserve well in advance. Closed November–March.

Sant Jaume €€ *Carrer Sant Jaume 6, tel: 971 549 419, fax: 971 897 255, <www.hotelsantjaume.com>*. Close to the city walls, this hotel occupies a 19th-century manor house, furnished in keeping with the period. It has a pretty patio with a fountain, and an open fireplace to cheer up winter evenings.

Formentor

Formentor €€€€ *Platja de Formentor s/n, tel: 971 899 100, fax: 971 865 155, <www.hotelformentor.net>*. This classic hotel was inaugurated in 1929 and guests have included film stars, world leaders and business magnates. The garden terraces are spectacular, as are the beach and views. Three swimming pools, three restaurants, beauty centre. Closed mid-January–mid-February.

Pollença

Juma €€ *Plaça Major 9, tel: 971 535 002, fax: 971 534 155, <www.hoteljuma.com>*. This small, smart hotel (only seven rooms), in a *Moderniste* building right on Pollença's picturesque plaza, has been keeping guests happy since 1907. Rooms are comfortable and slightly old-fashioned. There is a restaurant on the ground floor; breakfast is included in the price. Closed November–March.

La Posada de Lluc €€€ *Carrer Roser Vell 11, tel: 971 535 220, fax: 971 535 222, <www.posadalluc.com>.* An elegant, minimalist hotel with a small courtyard, close to the Sant Domingo complex. All eight rooms are individually decorated. The obliging owner/ manager is running a newish establishment and is keen to give good service.

Port de Pollença
Mar Calma € *Carreterra Formentor s/n, tel: 971 866 673, fax: 971 867 244.* A basic but functional hotel on a busy corner, one street back from the sea. No frills, and somewhat antiquated plumbing, but agreeable and helpful staff make it a good budget choice.

Miramar €€ *Passeig Anglada Camarasa 39, tel: 971 866 400, fax: 971 867 211.* An attractive and long-established beachfront hotel in the centre of town. The terrace has magnificent views of the bay and Cap de Formentor. The rooms have balconies but not all of them face the beach, so check when you make your booking. Closed November–March.

Sins Pins €€ *Passeig Anglada Camarasa 77, tel: 971 867 050, fax: 971 866 264.* This pretty, green-shuttered hotel with friendly staff is right on the beach. The bad news is that many rooms, especially those with sea-view balconies, are booked by tour operators or repeat customers. Worth a try, though.

THE EAST & SOUTHEAST

Artà
Ca'n Moragues €€€ *Carrer Pou Nou 12, Artà, tel: 971 829 509, fax: 971 829 530.* An 19th-century house tastefully converted into an extremely pleasant small hotel, with an attractive courtyard, a solarium, gym and indoor pool. Breakfast included. About 10km (6 miles) from the beach.

Casal d'Artà €€ *Carrer Rafael Blanes 19, tel/fax: 971 829 163.*
A family-run hotel in centre of town opposite a shady square. It
has some *Moderniste* features, including good stained glass.
Well-furnished throughout; some rooms have four-poster beds.
Solarium and roof terrace. Only 8 rooms, all with baths.

Sant Salvador €€€ *Carrer Castellet 7, Artà, tel: 971 829 555,
fax: 971 829 598.* A 19th-century manor house in the upper town
with a *Moderniste* exterior; each of the eight bedrooms is furnished
in individual style. Pool; several golf courses nearby. The restaurant, Ca'n Epifanio, is highly regarded *(see page 142).*

Cala d'Or
Cala d'Or €€ *Avinguda Bélgica 33, tel: 971 657 249, fax: 971
659 351, <www.hotelcalador.com>.* Attractively situated amid
pine trees, this elegant hotel overlooks an almost private cove. It
has an established reputation and friendly staff. Facilities include
pool, terraces, restaurant and beach bar. Excellent value. Closed
November–Easter.

Cala Figuera
Villa Sirena € *Carrer Virgen del Carmen 37, tel: 971 645 303,
fax: 971 645 106, <www.hotelvillasirena.com>.* A modern hotel set
right by the sea at the edge of this pretty village. Swimming pool.
Good value. No credit cards. Closed November–March.

Cala Ratjada
Cala Ratjada € *Carrer Miguel Garau 2, tel: 971 563 202, fax:
971 818 025.* A pleasant little *hostal* right by the port, with bright
yellow shutters; en suite rooms, some with small balconies; friendly proprietor. Good budget choice.

Ses Rotges €€€ *Carrer Rafael Blanes 21, Cala Ratjada, tel: 971
563 108, fax: 971 564 345, <www.sesrotges.com>.* A little oasis of
calm in this busy resort, owned and operated by a husband and wife
team who believe in personal service. The excellent restaurant has
earned a Michelin star. Not suitable for small children. Closed mid-
November to mid-March, but open for Christmas–New Year.

THE INTERIOR & CENTRAL PLAIN

Binissalem

Scott's Hotel €€€ *Plaça del Església, tel: 971 870 100, fax: 971 870 267,* <www.scotthotel.com>. An elegant and comfortable English-run hotel in an 18th-century mansion. Large beds and pure cotton sheets are among the pleasures. There's also a well-regarded restaurant, Scott's Bistro, tel: 971 870 076.

Randa

Es Reco de Randa €€€–€€€€ *Carrer Font 21 (4km/2½ miles from Algaida), tel: 971 660 997, fax: 971 662 558.* A delightful rural hotel in a manor house, just east of Palma. Facilities include pool, sauna, sun terrace, and an exceptional restaurant. The views are excellent, too. Book well in advance because it is popular.

Sineu

Celler de Ca'n Font € *Sa Plaça 18, tel: 971 520 295, fax: 971 520 301.* Just 7 rooms, simple but comfortable and air-conditioned, in this old house, which also runs a good restaurant.

León de Sineu €€€ *Carrer dels Bous 129, tel: 971 520 211, fax: 971 855 058,* <www.hotel-leondesineu.com>. An elegant, antique-furnished hotel, close to the central square in this attractive old town. Welcoming atmosphere and a good restaurant, Sa Boveda; swimming pool and garden.

Sa Bassa Rotja €€€ *Finca Son Orell, Camino Sa Pedrera s/n, Porreres, tel: 971 168 225, fax: 971 166 563,* <www.sabassarotja. com>. A 13th-century country mansion with indoor and outdoor pools, tennis courts, gym, solarium and a restaurant using locally produced ingredients. Ideal for a relaxed short break.

Son Bernadinet €€ *Carretera Campos–Porreres Km 5.9, tel: 971 181 650/971 186 149, fax: 971 186 043.* A lovely manor house hotel, surrounded by almond orchards, with a pool and gardens, and a log fire in winter. It feels miles from anywhere, but it's only 15 minutes' drive to the nearest beach.

Recommended Restaurants

Even if you are on an all-inclusive holiday, it is worth deserting your hotel dining room occasionally to discover what the island cuisine is like. The choice of restaurants ranges from up-market and elegant to informal establishments with an emphasis on good country cooking – *cuina mallorquina (see page 96)*. You will also find a plethora of tapas bars, especially in Palma, where you can have an adventurous and inexpensive meal. Local people eat late – lunch rarely begins till after 2pm and in the evening restaurants are at their busiest around 10–11pm. However, they all open much earlier in the evening, usually by 8pm, and those catering mainly to the northern European tourist market often stay open all afternoon. The *menú del día*, a three-course meal with wine included, is an inexpensive option, although it is often only available at lunchtime.

The following basic price guide (which is only approximate) is for a three-course *à la carte* meal for one, with house wine:

€€€€	over 70 euros
€€€	40–70 euros
€€	25–40 euros
€	below 25 euros

PALMA

Caballito del Mar €€ *Passeig de Sagrera 5, tel: 971 721 074.* The place to go for fresh fish and shellfish cooked to suit your own particular requirements. There's an outside terrace just around the corner from lively Plaça Sa Llotja, but unfortunately it is separated from the waterfront by the busy main road.

Ca'n Carlos €€ *Carrer de S'Aigua 5, tel: 971 713 869.* On a quiet pedestrian street, this atmospheric place specialises in authentic *cuina mallorquina*. Dishes include roast lamb and aubergine stuffed with shellfish. Closed Sunday and second week of August.

Celler Sa Premsa € *Plaça Bisbe Berenguer de Palou 8, tel: 971 723 529.* This Mallorcan dining hall is a real Palma institution and is very popular. Serves good, filling, everyday food with a wide selection of Mallorcan classic dishes. Great ambience and reasonable prices. Closed Saturday and Sunday.

El Pesquero € *Moll de la Llotja s/n, Port de Palma, tel: 971 715 220.* A variety of fish and seafood dishes served on a broad deck overlooking the port. Cheerful atmosphere. Many people come here just for an early evening drink and a portion of tapas.

Firol Restaurante € *Carrer Apuntadors 3, tel: 971 716 610.* Always busy and vibrant, the Firol has a vast range of excellent tapas – and the portions are pretty big, too. Try the *pimientos de padrón.* Ground floor and basement dining rooms.

Koldo Royo €€€ *Avinguda Ingeniero Gabriel Roca 3 (Passeig Marítim), tel: 971 732 435.* Considered by many to be Palma's best restaurant, this small, elegant place overlooks the waterfront. The eponymous Basque chef creates imaginative delicacies such as canneloni stuffed with aubergine and prawns. Closed Sunday; call to check on occasional/summer closures.

La Bóveda €–€€ *Carrer Botería 3, tel: 971 714 863.* There's usually a queue of tourists outside at 8pm each evening, waiting for the door to open, but this big, lively place is equally popular with locals, who come later. There's a wide selection of excellent tapas and main courses. Another branch, with more modern decor, is found at *Passeig Sagrera 3, tel: 971 720 026.* Both closed Sunday.

La Lonja € *Carrer Lonja del Mar 2, tel: 971 722 799.* With a wood-panelled dining room and tables out in the Plaça Sa Llonja (café, street and square use Catalan and Spanish spellings interchangeably), this unassuming place has good and reasonably priced tapas, and the square is a great place to sit and enjoy them.

La Paloma € *Carrer Apuntadors 16, tel: 971 721 745.* In the heart of the eating quarter, La Paloma has no outside tables, but the dining room is cool and pleasant, the staff attentive. Reasonable food at reasonable prices. The *gazpacho* is good.

Porto Pí €€€–€€€€ *Avinguda Joan Miró, 174 y Garita, 25, tel: 971 400 087.* Hidden away by the port below Bellver Castle, this old Mallorcan house has a Michelin star. International dishes are prepared using fresh local ingredients and plenty of imaginative flair. Closed Saturday lunchtime and Sunday.

THE WESTERN CORNER

Andratx
Mirador Ricardo Roca € *Carretera Andratx–Estellencs, tel: 971 618 527.* The recommendation is for the setting rather than the food, which is only average. Perched on the cliff top, the views makes it a spectacular place to have lunch, or just stop for a drink.

Banyalbufar
Son Tomás €€ *Carrer Baronia 17, tel: 971 618 149.* A small bar-restaurant with a terrace commanding outstanding views of the coast. Fresh fish comes directly from the boats in the cove; the paella and the *arroz negro* (black rice) are recommended. Closed Tuesday and November–February.

THE WEST COAST

Deià
Ca'n Quet €€–€€€ *Carretera Valledemossa–Deià, tel: 971 639 196.* This renowned restaurant, linked to the hotel Es Molí *(see page 130),* specialises in international cuisine with a local flavour. Popular with Mallorcans, who flock from Palma for dishes such as giant prawns in puff pastry. Closed Monday and November–April.

El Barrigon € *Archiduc Lluis Salvador 13, tel: 971 639 139.* Loud and lively, this popular place on the main road specialises in tapas and they come in all varieties. The stuffed squid is extremely good; the staff are friendly and casual; there's an outside terrace open in summer.

El Olivo €€€–€€€€ *Son Canals, tel: 971 639 011.* One of the top restaurants on the island, attached to La Residencia Hotel *(see page 131).* Delicious nouvelle cuisine is prepared under the watchful eye of a French chef. Try his gastronomic menu if you feel flush. It would be difficult to top the experience of dining on the terrace for sheer romance. The wine cellar is excellent. Open daily for dinner only.

Es Racó d'es Teix €€€ *Carrer Sa Vinya Veia 6, tel: 971 639 501.* Chef Josef Saueschell produces nouvelle cuisine in satisfying portions. The *ballontine conejo* (medallions of rabbit) is delicious. The food and the fairytale gardens with ravishing views make it easy to forgive the fact that it's a tad pretentious.

Jaume €€€ *Archiduc Lluis Salvador 24, tel: 971 639 029.* Family-owned and operated for over three decades, this friendly place prepares generous helpings of authentic Mallorcan food. Book if you want to eat on the terrace. Go for fresh seafood and classics like *tumbet (see page 97).* Dinner only; closed Monday.

Sóller

El Guía €€ *Carrer Castanyer 3, tel: 971 630 227.* In Sóller's nicest hotel *(see page 132),* a small, well-run family restaurant producing typical Mallorcan dishes, for which the perfect accompaniment is Binissalem wine. Good-value *menú del día.* Closed Monday.

Sa Cova €€ *Plaça Constitució 7, Sóller, tel: 971 633 222.* Pleasant restaurant on the square. Serves good *conejo* (rabbit), which appears on many menus in the area, and seafood stew – *cazuela.*

Ses Porxeres €€–€€€ *Carretera Palma–Soller, Km17, Bunyola, tel: 971 613 762.* A beautiful Catalan restaurant near the Jardins d'Àlfabia. Specialities include game, fish stews and lamb cutlets grilled on hot rocks at your table. Reservations essential, especially for Sunday lunch. Closed Sunday evening, Monday and August.

Valldemossa

Sa Cartoixa € *Plaça Ramón Llull 5, tel: 971 616 059.* Large traditional restaurant with seating inside and out, close to the monastery.

Dishes include *tumbet (see page 97)* and stuffed peppers. Can get busy with tour groups at lunchtime.

THE NORTH

Cala Sant Vicenç
Cavall Bernat €€€ *Carrer Maressers 2, tel: 971 530 250*. An excellent restaurant in the Cala Sant Vicenç hotel *(see page 133)*. Refined Mediterranean cooking and a fine wine list. There's a set menu of delicious tastes, interspersed with sorbet. Open daily for dinner; closed December–January.

Pollença
Clivia €€ *Avinguda Pollentia 7, Pollença, tel: 971 533 635/971 534 616*. An elegant lace-curtained setting in which to enjoy Mallorcan cuisine – fish soup, baked *lubina* (sea bass) and mountain ham are favourites. Closed Tuesday lunchtime.

Il Giardino €€ *Plaça Major 11, Pollença, tel: 971 534 302*. Great Italian food served in a pleasant dining room and outside on the square, where you must book to get a table. Sunday lunch here is a social occasion.

Trencadora €€ *Carrer Ramon Llull 7, Pollença; tel: 971 531 859*. Open all year. In summer you can eat on the terrace, in a courtyard garden or airy indoor dining room. Organic products are used whenever possible. Mediterranean style food, with good value set menus.

Port de Pollença
Stay €€–€€€ *Moll Nou s/n, tel: 971 864 013*. A smart restaurant right in the centre of the port that has been operating for years. Fish is the first choice but there are imaginative meat dishes too, especially lamb. A set menu features both. Open every day of the year.

Tribeca €€ *Carretera Formentor 43, tel: 971 866 423*. Prides itself on a varied menu using fresh local ingredients. Wild mushrooms, stuffed aubergines and local trout feature. Vegetarian dishes always available. Open all year for dinner.

THE EAST AND SOUTHEAST

Artà
Ca'n Epifanio €€–€€€ *Carrer Castellet 7, tel: 971 829 555*. In the Sant Salvador hotel this restaurant has a small, frequently changing menu, including such goodies as *mille feuille* of lobster.

Cala d'Or
Le Mirage €€€ *Porto Cari, Local 07-09, tel: 971 643 483*. Of an eclectic row of restaurants lining the harbour, this is a smart choice. The well-presented dishes include medallions of *rape* (monkfish) and mussel risotto.

Cala Ratjada
Ses Rotjes €€€–€€€€ *Carrer Rafael Blanes 21, tel: 971 563 108*. This restaurant, in the hotel of the same name, has a Michelin star and is a delightful find. Although fresh fish is their speciality, they don't neglect the meat dishes. The extensive wine list is not over-priced. You can eat in a sheltered courtyard in summer. Reservations advisable. Closed mid-November–mid-March.

THE CENTRAL PLAIN

Inca
Celler Ca'n Amer €€ *Carrer Pau 39, tel: 971 501 261*. The best known of Inca's famous *cellers*, this family-run establishment has a long tradition of serving large portions of robust island food and a vast selection of wines.

Petra
Es Celler €€ *Carrer de l'Hospital 46, tel: 971 561 056*. Huge and cavernous restaurant serving heaped plates of traditional food.

Sineu
Celler de Ca'n Font €€ *Sa Plaça, Sineu, tel: 971 520 313*. Another one of the traditional *cellers*, Ca'n Font, in a hotel of the same name *(see page 136)*, specialises in *sopas mallorquinas*, roast suckling pig and rice dishes.

INDEX